LEVEL ONE

More than Words

LIVING FAITH BIBLE CURRICULUM

REBECCA SPOONER

Master Books®
A Division of New Leaf Publishing Group
www.masterbooks.com

Author: Rebecca Spooner

Master Books Creative Team:

Editor: Craig Froman

Design: Jennifer Bauer

Cover Design: Diana Bogardus

Copy Editors:
Judy Lewis
Willow Meek

Curriculum Review:
Laura Welch
Diana Bogardus

First printing: September 2019
Fifth printing: August 2020

Master Books® is a division of the New Leaf Publishing Group, Inc.

ISBN: 978-1-68344-162-5
ISBN: 978-1-61458-719-4 (digital)
Library of Congress Number: 2019941928

Unless otherwise noted, Scripture quotations are from the English Standard Version (ESV) of the Bible.

Printed in the United States of America

Please visit our website for other great titles:
www.masterbooks.com

All artwork from istock.com or shutterstock.com except page 226 (Superstock.com) and pages 16, 40, 72, 94, 118, 142, 172, 196, 250, 274 (Public Domain.)

About the Author

Rebecca Spooner is a homeschooling mom of five young children who was homeschooled herself. She lives in Northern British Columbia with her husband, her children, her many homeschool books, and her coffee maker. She spends her days blogging, writing books, recording videos and podcasts, speaking at homeschool conventions, and raising her children. She is a worship leader at her church and is passionate about helping to inspire a generation of children who know who they are and who have a personal, life-changing relationship with God.

To the teacher,

Welcome to *More Than Words* — a journey for the whole family! This book is written to the child and filled with 36 weeks of stories, activities, poems, hymns, character studies, art, picture studies, word studies, and more. Like a good piece of dark chocolate, every tiny nibble is packed with flavor to provide a rich learning experience.

This curriculum was born through a need. As a homeschool mom of five young kids, I was searching for a Bible program that went beyond Bible stories. I wanted to raise up my kids to have a firm foundation in their faith. After searching through the current market for something that was easy to understand and yet not afraid to tackle these deeper topics, I felt compelled to write something of my own.

More Than Words is divided into four units.

1. The first unit is all about who God is. Children will be learning about some of the attributes of God.

2. The second unit is about who we are in God. This unit goes into basic theology of the Roman road: we are fallen and imperfect, we fall short, we are redeemed by grace and saved through faith, and we are called and set apart for a purpose. In a culture that is so filled with confusion, I am determined that my children discover their identity in Christ — one that cannot be taken away or shaken by opinion or culture.

3. The third unit goes into what it means to be a Christian.

4. The last unit is how to walk out their faith in the day-to-day real life that they face.

Make sure you read the "How to Use This Book" section to understand the various sections. You will need one book per child and can do this on an individual basis, with the whole family together, or even in a classroom or Sunday school setting.

My heart was to create something beautiful, a morning basket in a book — something to take the pressure off the teacher and yet captivate and draw the child into deeper connection and relationship with Jesus. May each book that is put in the hands of a child be anointed with the revelation power of God. It is my prayer that it will be a tool, a part of the firm foundation of a new generation; that it be an instigator, a catalyst even, to help a child make their faith their own — not their parents, not just something they do or talk about, but something they believe, something that shapes their identity and values.

May these pages be used by God for His glory and purposes.

Rebecca Spooner

Suggested Daily Schedule
Quarter 1: Who Is God?

Quarter 2: Who Am I to God?

Quarter 4: The Great Relationship

JOURNAL ENTRY

Malakai and Aliyah begin various weeks with a journal entry that helps students relate to that week's teaching. Some of these are from their real experiences and some are made up for the book.

TALK ABOUT IT!

This will connect readers to the journals and other teachings in the book. Feel free to have younger students speak the answer to the teacher, while older students can write it out if they wish.

CHECK IT WITH THE WORD!

The Bible says that we should test everything through the Word of God, that means that everything we read and hear, even our own thoughts, need to be checked with the Bible. We'll be doing this every week!

KEY TRUTH

Every week we are going to write down one important thing that we are learning, called our key truth, and at the end of the week we will often put it into our journal, so try to remember it while you write it!

CHARACTER STUDY

Character studies are built in in a very relational way. Each week will have a brief discussion of a character trait and how it ties into the Bible, our faith, and our Christian walk. Optional extension activities are built in with word studies (for older students to begin to understand synonyms and antonyms and have more context for the word) and flashcards to enhance the lessons. These are not required and are explained further on.

COPYWORK

Copywork: Each week students will be copying certain verses of the Bible that help them better understand the truth of each lesson. Copying and writing things helps us remember them better. That means it is so important to write out the Scriptures to help us learn them and better apply them to our lives. If the verses are too long for the student's stamina or ability, the teacher may copy part of the verse, leaving key words for the student to write according to their ability.

FLASH CARD FUN

Flashcards are creative ways to learn. And because the character traits are so important, you'll be creating these each week and using them for reviews. Use 3 x 5 cards or any other format you wish to write the information on, then feel free to design them with your own artistic flair! Make it optional if you like!

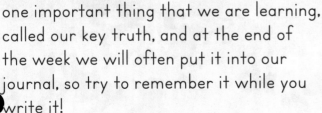

HYMN STUDY, ART STUDY, POEM STUDY

We'll be exploring hymns, poems, and artwork on various weeks, learning what they mean and how they help us learn about teachings in God's Word.

WORD STUDY

Word studies are created specifically for older students, teaching them more about the word meanings, as well as synonyms and antonyms in the process. You can learn more about a word by finding similar words, just like you can learn more about something by looking at things that are opposite of it.

COLOR IT, DRAW IT

These are times to color or draw an image that is based often on the character study or key truths. Everything in the lessons is designed to build on the key teachings.

JOURNAL

This journaling time can be for older students who can write out their responses, or for younger students who share or narrate their responses to their teachers. This section helps bring the week's lesson to a close.

QUARTERLY REVIEWS

The week at the end of each quarter is used as a review time. Keep student flashcards handy and enjoy this time looking back over the prior lessons, all that God's Word has taught you.

COURSE SUPPLY LIST

There are a few items you will want to have handy each week, which include:

☐ colored pencils or crayons
☐ a pencil or marker
☐ and scissors.

A few items throughout the course are used for optional projects, which would include:

☐ 3 x 5 index cards
☐ stickers
☐ journal
☐ highlighters
☐ post-it notes
☐ tape
☐ poster board
☐ paint
☐ paint brushes

QUARTER 1:
Who Is God?

Let's get started!

This is a special book. Your parent or teacher probably bought it because they wanted you to learn more about the Bible and who God is. It is your very own, very special journal, and in it you will be reading through two kids' journals who are the same age (or close to the same age) as you are! I wrote about my son, Malakai, who is 8, and my daughter, Aliyah (Ah-lee-yah), who is 6. They are real kids, and some of the stories and journal entries in this book are real, some of them I made up.

Most of the time, kids don't read the introductions to their school books. Those are written to your parents or teachers, but like I said, this book is special! It isn't a book for an adult. It is a journal all for you to help you document your journey with Jesus and learn more about who God is, who YOU are in God, and what it means to be a Christian and live a life that can change the world!

He loves you SO, SO much, and I know that He is just as excited as you are that you are starting this journey to learn more about Him.

So every time it's Bible time, every time you pull this special book out, I want you to think of it a little bit differently than your other school work. This book is full of stories and coloring and drawing and beautiful paintings and poetry, and you'll be creating your very own journal of what God is teaching you this year!

I'm so excited to have you join me and my kids, and I can't wait to see and hear about your journal when you are done!

Happy adventuring with Malakai and Aliyah!

Rebecca Spooner

(I'm the writer, and Malakai and Aliyah's mom!)

Today mom bought me a journal to use for school. She told me that I could write about what I do and what I learn and what I am thinking about so that I can remember when I am older. We went to church and Mrs. Drycke (our Sunday school teacher) told us about something called "The Trinity." She said that it meant that God was three people, but all one God. She drew a triangle to show that even though there are three different sides — the Holy Spirit, God the Father, and Jesus the Son — they are all God. Jesus died for us on the Cross and He took our sin, so He actually conquered death! Hi-yah! God is our Father up in heaven. He created everything just by talking! And the Holy Spirit can talk to us and help us and is always with us, and He is our friend who never leaves us!

Malakai

Father TRINITY Son
GOD
Holy Spirit

Trinity means 3. Do you remember the three people who are God?

What other power do you think God has?

Check it with the Word!
BIBLE

The Bible says that we should test everything through the Word of God. That means that everything we read and hear, even our own thoughts, need to be compared (or checked) with the Bible to make sure it is true. Not everything we read or hear or think is true, so turn in your Bible to John 14:26 and let's read together. Your Bible might be a little bit different than mine, so you can read in your own if you prefer:

> But the Helper, the Holy Spirit, whom the Father will send in my name, he will teach you all things and bring to your remembrance all that I have said to you. (John 14:26)

In this verse, Jesus is speaking about the Holy Spirit being sent by the Father in heaven. It shows us all three persons of God in one verse. Isn't that cool?

Copy the Key Truth on the lines.

KEY TRUTH:

God is 3 in 1

God is 3 in 1

Copywork: Did you know that copying and writing things can help us remember? Every week, we are going to copy a Bible verse to help us learn more about who God is and what He says.

But the Helper, the Holy Spirit...
will teach you all things... (John 14:26)

Name: _____

Day: 1 ② 3 4

The Holy Trinity by Luca Rossetti da Orta (1738-1739)

LET'S TALK ABOUT IT!

1. This painting was done by an artist named Luca Rossetti da Orta. What is the setting of the painting (where they are)? (the clouds / up in the sky)

2. Do you notice the rings of light coming up from the three of them? What do you think that means? (answers may vary)

3. There are lots of symbols used in this painting, like the cross behind Jesus, or Jesus with holes in his feet and hands. These help us get a better picture of what the artist meant and are called symbolism. Do you notice the triangle around God's head? Do you know what that means? Do you remember what a triangle shows us? (God is three persons in one, or the Trinity).

Art study

WEEK 1: THE TRINITY

16

CHARACTER STUDY

HUMBLE

Sometimes we have reasons to be proud of ourselves and what we have done (like being really good at reading or playing a sport). To be humble means that you aren't showing off. It's kind of like lowering yourself instead of thinking of yourself as better than people and making them feel bad. The Bible talks about clothing ourselves with humility.

Today I am going to teach you a new word — synonym.

A synonym just means that it has the same meaning as another word. Finding synonyms can help us have a better understanding of a word.

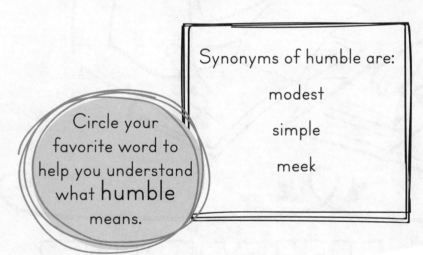

Circle your favorite word to help you understand what **humble** means.

Synonyms of humble are:

modest

simple

meek

Flash Card FUN

Make a flashcard with this week's character trait on it and decorate it however you want!

WEEK 1: THE TRINITY

Name: _____

Day: 1 2 3 ④

draw it!

Each week, you have space to draw a picture, paint, or even use stickers or pieces of paper to illustrate (show) what you are learning about. In the space below, draw something that comes to mind when you think of God. This might be something God created, or it might be Jesus healing someone who was sick, or it might be the Holy Spirit in the form of the dove that came down on Jesus when he was baptized.

WEEK 1: THE TRINITY

journal!

Each week there is a space for you to do some writing and to answer some questions to help you get started. If you aren't able to write yet, that's okay! A parent or teacher can write down your thoughts for you. Writing is all about getting our thoughts and words out on paper, so you are still writing even if you don't hold the pencil (cool, huh?).

This week, you learned about God being three and yet one. That is called "The Trinity." This year, you are going to be learning more about all three persons of God — the Father, the Son (Jesus), and the Holy Spirit. Write a little something about what you remember from this week.

NOT ON MY OWN STRENGTH...

Thank You, God, for teaching me to be humble, to not brag or show off but to care about other people.

Today was a hard day. I banged my knee, and it is purple and bruised and it still hurts. Malakai was making armor with some big boxes while Janiah (my sister) and I were dancing. I tripped over one of his boxes and hit my knee on the coffee table. I was so mad at him! Mom told me that I have to love my brother even when he makes me mad and act in a loving way to him. But it was REALLY hard because I was still angry and my knee still hurt. I asked Jesus to help me forgive him, and Malakai said he was sorry he had left his boxes out. We hugged each other and even though my knee still hurts, I am not angry at him anymore. God loves me so much that I have enough love to share with my family and friends, and I can ask Him to help me when it is hard!

Aliyah

Name:  _____

Day: ① 2 3 4

talk about it!

Have you ever been angry at someone?

Did that make it hard to forgive them and act in a loving way to them?

What can you do when it feels hard to be loving?

Check it with the Word!

BIBLE

Turn to 1 John 4:7–8 in your Bible and read with me:

> Beloved, let us love one another, for love is from God, and whoever loves has been born of God and knows God. Anyone who does not love does not know God, because God is love.

In this verse, we learn that all love comes from God! He is the source of the love that we feel, the love that we give and receive. Every time we feel love, God is in it! The more time we spend with God, the more we know Him, and the more we know and can show God's love to other people, too! Isn't that cool?

KEY TRUTH:

God is love

God is love

_____
- - - - - - - - - - - - - - -
_____
_____
- - - - - - - - - - - - - - -
_____

Copywork: The Bible tells us in Deuteronomy 11:18 that we should write the Word of God on our hearts and souls. That means that when we write out the Bible, we want to say the words and think about them WHILE we write them so that we aren't just writing on the paper, we are writing them on our hearts. So get your heart, mind, and pencil ready to write this week's verse!

Beloved, let us love one another,
for love is from God... 1 John 4:7

Name: _____

HYMN STUDY

Read these lyrics out loud slowly and think about the words.

Overview: This song is all about the love of God being so much bigger than we could ever understand. His love is ALWAYS there for us.

THE LOVE OF GOD

Hymn: verse one	Interpretation:
The love of God is greater far	The love of God is better
Than tongue or pen can ever tell	Than anyone can say or write
It goes beyond the highest star	It is higher than the stars
And reaches to the lowest hell	Always there no matter how far away from God you are
The guilty pair, bowed down with care	For everyone that is guilty
God gave His Son to win	God gave His Son, Jesus, to defeat sin
His erring child He reconciled	God's sinful child (us) He made right again
And pardoned from his sin	And forgave his sin

What is your favorite line in the song?

Go back and highlight it or underline it.

talk about it!

You can explore this entire hymn with a line-by-line modern interpretation in the appendices on pages 297-298.

WEEK 2: GOD IS LOVE

CONTENT

Can you tell your parent or teacher what it means to be content?

To be content is to be thankful in your circumstances, with what you have or where you are or even how old you are. Today, we are going to learn a new word. It is called an antonym. An antonym is a word that has the opposite meaning. An antonym of content is to be unhappy or jealous. Instead of being thankful for where you are or what you have, you think about how everything could be better if only you had something else.

Narrate to your teacher or write some things you have thought would make you happy if you had them.

_____
- -
_____
- -
_____

Did having them keep you always happy? True contentment is found in God. What do you think that means?

Here are three words that are synonyms for the word **content**. Write your favorite one on the line.

joyful, peaceful, at ease

_____

Flash Card FUN
Make a flashcard with this week's character trait on it and decorate it however you want!

25

WEEK 2: GOD IS LOVE

I AM CONTENT

draw it!

Draw a picture of a time when you were loving to someone or they were loving to you. Or draw any picture that shows a story of love because that is kind of like a picture of God . . . God is love!

WEEK 2: GOD IS LOVE

journal!

Can you remember our key truth for the week?
(Look back for the key if you can't remember.):

What is one thing you can be content about?

NOT ON MY OWN STRENGTH...

God, thank You that you have given
me SO much! Thank You that
You take care of me. Help me to
remember everything You have done
for me and to be more content.

I drove my motorbike today. I love my motorbike. I always have to wear my helmet and I have to make sure mom or dad is watching and put it away after. They give me rules about driving my motorbike because they say I am crazy and wild. I like to drive fast! I haven't ever fallen and gotten hurt though because my dad has lots of rules. Sometimes I don't like rules, but my friend, Tim, fell off his bike one time and got really hurt, so I guess I am glad my dad watches out for me. It's kind of like how God watches out for me. My Sunday school teacher, Mrs. Drycke, told me that God is always good. Even when my life seems kind of bad, it doesn't change that God is good. She said it is part of His character, I guess that means who He is. When I think about my motorbike, it helps me remember that God is good because I am pretty happy that I get to drive it even though I am only 8. I am going to start looking for other things that show me that God is good. I wonder what I'll find. . . .

Malakai

Name: _____

Day: ① 2 3 4

talk
about it!

Can you think of some rules your parents have to keep you safe?

What is something in your life that reminds you that God is good?

Check it
with the
Word!

BIBLE

Let's see if we can find the Book of James. It's in the New Testament, after the gospels (those are the books of the Bible that tell about Jesus' life — Matthew, Mark, Luke, and John). Found it? Look for chapter 1:17 and read along with me:

Every good gift and every perfect gift is from above, coming down from the Father of lights, with whom there is no variation or shadow due to change.

God is so good that EVERYTHING good and perfect comes from Him, and that never changes. He never changes. He is good ALL the time, every day, in every circumstance. Every good thought you have, every good idea, every blessing in your life (like food and clothing and that new toy your parents got you) comes from Him. He is a good God, and He is the giver of good gifts! Let's read one more Bible verse to help us see and recognize God's goodness all around us. Turn to Matthew 7:11 (the very first book in the New Testament).

If you then, who are evil, know how to give good gifts to your children, how much more will your Father who is in heaven give good things to those who ask him!

If your mommy and daddy know how to give good gifts, then how much more does God? We can trust that He has goodness in store for us, and even when we have hard days, He can use that for good things in our lives.

KEY
TRUTH:

God is good

God is good

_____
- - - - - - - - - - - - - - - -
_____
_____
- - - - - - - - - - - - - - - -
_____

Copywork:
Remember, we aren't just writing this with our hand, we want to write it on our hearts! So say the words while you write them, think about them while you write them, and let it sink in. Like water sinks into soil, God's words can sink into our hearts and change us! God's Word is powerful!

Every good gift and every perfect gift is from above, coming down from the Father of lights. . . .(James 1:17)

WEEK 3: GOD IS GOOD

Name: _____

Day: 1 ② 3 4

Read this poem about
God's goodness.
Watch for certain
patterns in the
lines and words.

Poetry

I know that God is good
Even when my day is not.
I know that God is good
Even when things go bad a lot.

I know that God is good
By the beauty that I see.
I know that God is good
Creation speaks His majesty.

I know that God is good
When I am thankful for what I have.
I know that God is good
He paid the price on my behalf.

I know that God is good
No matter what anyone says.
I know that God is good
Because it's who He is.

talk
about it!

Did you find the patterns? It has a pattern in the way it
looks — it has four lines and then a space, can you see that?
It also has a pattern in the way it sounds. Did you hear any
rhyming words in the poem? Go back and read it one more
time, and this time, can you highlight, circle, or underline
every word that rhymes?

WEEK 3: GOD IS GOOD

32

CHARACTER STUDY

DEPENDABLE

Do you know what it means to be dependable? It means people can depend on you; they can trust you to be there for them or to do what you say you will do. It means you are reliable, kind of like how we don't have to question or wonder if a chair will do its job. We just jump over and sit on it, totally trusting that it will be sturdy and strong and hold us up. That's kind of like being dependable . . . and it is a good character trait that we can work on and develop to become even more like Jesus who is dependable and who we can always trust.

Now that we know what a synonym is (has similar meaning) and what an antonym is (has opposite meaning), we can use those to help us understand more about what **dependable** means. Circle the synonyms of dependable below and cross out the antonyms.

faithful

uncertain

dishonest

DEPENDABLE

loyal

reliable

disloyal

Flash Card FUN

Make a flashcard with this week's character trait on it and decorate it however you want!

WEEK 3: GOD IS GOOD

33

Name:

Day: 1 2 ③ 4

color it!

I AM DEPENDABLE

draw it!

Draw a picture that reminds you of God's goodness. Maybe it is something good like your family, maybe it is a picture of something in nature you saw on a nature walk, or maybe it is something He did for you. If you can't think of something, ask a parent or teacher or even ask God to help you think of some ways He has been good to you. God is really good at showing us His nature, or who He is, when we ask Him!

WEEK 3: GOD IS GOOD

journal!

Can you remember our key truth for the week? (Look back for the key if you can't remember.):

_____
- - - - - - - - - - - - - - - - - - - -
_____
_____
- - - - - - - - - - - - - - - - - - - -
_____

You can be more dependable by doing what you say you will do, even if you change your mind or get distracted. What is one thing you can do this week that will help you to be more dependable?

_____
- - - - - - - - - - - - - - - - - - - -
_____
_____
- - - - - - - - - - - - - - - - - - - -
_____
_____
- - - - - - - - - - - - - - - - - - - -
_____

NOT ON MY OWN STRENGTH...

Thank You, Father, for showing me such a good example of someone I can depend on. You are always there for me. Help me to be there for other people when they need me, too.

It is Malakai's birthday soon, and mom went shopping for his birthday present. I wish it was my birthday, but my birthday isn't for a long, long, LONG time. Mom told me about when I was born. I love hearing that story because that was my very first day and I don't even remember it! I'm going to ask my mom when God's birthday is. I know that Jesus' birthday is why we celebrate Christmas, but what about God?

I'm back! Mom said that God (even Jesus) doesn't have a beginning or an end. It means He is eternal! He won't ever die and He was there even before the world was made! God is even bigger than time! I am learning about time in my math in school, and everything has time. I wonder what it would be like without time: seasons and morning and night time and months and years. God is even bigger than I thought He was!

Aliyah

Name: _____

Day: ① 2 3 4

talk about it!

When is your birthday?

Do you like talking about your first day and what you were like when you were a baby?

• • • • • • • • • • • • • • • •

BIBLE

Check it with the Word!

Let's turn to the middle of our Bibles to Psalm 90:2 and let's read together:

Before the mountains were brought forth, or ever you had formed the earth and the world, from everlasting to everlasting you are God.

Even though Jesus was born as a human baby and we celebrate that at Christmas, He was in heaven forever before that. Jesus, God, and the Holy Spirit have no beginning! They were here always and forever and will be here always and forever. They cannot die and they weren't born or made like we were. Part of God's character, part of who He is . . . is eternal.

KEY TRUTH:

God is eternal

God is eternal

_____

_____

_____

_____

Copywork: Let's write these words on the page and in our hearts!

Before the mountains were brought forth . . . you are God. (Psalm 90:2)

WEEK 4: GOD IS ETERNAL

Master Baby by Sir William Quiller Orchardson 1886

Today, we are going to study a painting of a baby to help us remember that while we have a beginning and an end, God does not. He was always there, from before the earth was even made! See how the baby is looking and reaching up?

LET'S LOOK CLOSER

This painting is oil on canvas. If you look closely, you can see the strokes of paint, especially on the baby's pillow and the wall behind them. Study the baby's feet. What do you notice? Follow the baby's gaze — what is he or she looking at? How does this painting make you feel? What kinds of colors do you see? Does the mother look happy? What is your favorite detail in this painting?

Art study

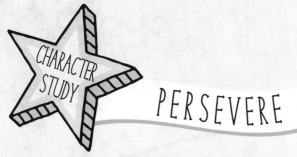

CHARACTER STUDY

PERSEVERE

Have you ever heard the word persevere? To persevere is a really important character quality. It means to not give up. The Bible talks to us a lot about persevering, probably because it is easier to give up when things seem hard or impossible. Kind of like when you are learning how to ride a bike. Sometimes you fall down a lot. It is frustrating and sometimes it even hurts! But you have to keep on trying to learn it because no one can do it for you! Every time you try when you feel like giving up, it helps you to grow your perseverance muscle! The Bible even says in James 1:2−3 that we should consider it JOY when we face hard times because it helps us learn to hold on.

Look at the first word in the row. Then, circle if the word is a synonym or antonym for the word **persevere**.

endure	synonym	antonym
quit	synonym	antonym
keep going	synonym	antonym
give up	synonym	antonym
hold on	synonym	antonym
stop	synonym	antonym

Flash Card FUN
Make a flashcard with this week's character trait on it and decorate it however you want!

41

Name:

Day: 1 2 ③ 4

color it!

I CAN PERSEVERE

draw it!

Can you draw a picture of the world as a black circle showing what it might have looked like before it was created? The Bible tells us it was dark and formless (Genesis 1:2). There was no moon or sun, no land or oceans, but even before the earth was created, God was there! Over the world, draw a picture of a dove to show the Spirit of God. (Remember how that is called symbolism, when a picture represents or stands for something?) Because God said, "the Spirit of God was hovering over the face of the waters" (Genesis 1:2), we are going to draw that to help us remember that God is bigger than time and that He was here before even the world was made!

WEEK 4: GOD IS ETERNAL

journal!

What is this week's key truth?

_____
. . . .
_____
_____
. . . .
_____

Write a sentence or two sharing your favorite thing you learned this week. Don't forget to start with a capital letter and end with a punctuation mark!

_____
. . . .
_____
_____
. . . .
_____
_____

NOT ON MY OWN STRENGTH . . .

Help me to be someone that doesn't give up or complain when things are hard. Thank You that You make me strong, God!

Today was so scary. I was at the store with my mom, and I saw this really cool remote control helicopter that had a camera in it! I was looking at it so closely that when I looked up, my mom was gone! I looked everywhere but couldn't find her! I was so scared, I went up and down a few aisles, but she wasn't there, either.

Mom always tells us to stay where we are if we are lost and she'll come find us. I felt alone until I remembered the Bible verse mom had taught me about God never leaving me, and so I said, "God is always with me." Then the coolest thing happened! I wasn't so scared anymore! I was sure that mom would find me soon, and I knew God loved me so much. Then mom came around the corner and gave me a big hug. She seemed relieved to find me and was just glad I was safe! I'm glad that God loves me enough to be with me even at the store!

Malakai

Name: _____

Day: ① 2 3 4

Have you ever felt alone or scared?

Why do you think Malakai saying "God is always with me" helped him not be scared?

Check it with the Word!

Open up your Bible to one of my favorite verses to read when I feel scared or lonely, Deuteronomy 31:6:

Be strong and courageous. Do not fear or be in dread of them, for it is the LORD your God who goes with you. He will not leave you or forsake you.

Do you know what forsake means? It means abandon. God will never leave you, never ever. And His Word, the Bible, isn't like any other book because the words aren't just words. The Word of God is also called the sword of the Spirit (Ephesians 6:17), and it is living and active, sharper than any sword, and it discerns the intention of the heart (Hebrews 4:12). The Bible also tells us that fear doesn't come from God (2 Timothy 1:7), so when we are afraid and we use the sword of the Spirit (the Word of God, the Bible), we battle against fear! Remind yourself not to be afraid, that God is with you, and that He will never leave you. This week, we are learning something about God that lets us know He is everywhere. God is always present, with everyone, everywhere, in the whole world! God is always with us!

KEY TRUTH:

God is always with me

God is always with me

_____

- - - - - - - - - - -

_____

- - - - - - - - - - -

_____

Name: _____

Day: 1 ②3 4

Copywork: Don't forget to read the words and think about them while you write out your Bible verse this week! You can even write this verse and put it over your bed to read when you have bad dreams!

Be strong and courageous. Do not fear or be in dread of them, for it is the LORD your God who goes with you... Deuteronomy 31:6

Overview: This hymn is based off of Psalm 23, a famous psalm. No matter what happens, God is leading us and will never leave us.

23rd PSALM

Hymn: verse four		Interpretation:
Yea, though I walk in death's dark vale,		Even when I am touched by death's shadow (maybe someone in your life dies)
Yet will I fear no ill:		I will fear nothing bad
For thou art with me, and thy rod		Because you are with me, and your rod
And staff comfort still.		And your staff (the tools of a shepherd) comfort me

talk about it!

This hymn is based off of a passage in the Bible that talks about God being with us, even when things seem dark and scary. It uses some old language that is a little bit hard to understand, but we can learn more by looking at it.

Can you find the line "For thou art with me" and circle it?
The part before it means even if I go through hard times, I won't be afraid because God is with me.

Can you think of a time when you were going through a hard time and God was with you?

You can explore this entire hymn with a line-by-line modern interpretation on pages 299-300.

WEEK 5: GOD IS EVERYWHERE

PATIENT

To be patient means to be able to wait. Whew, that is a HARD one! Even for adults that is really hard! We like to have things happen right now! Wouldn't it be nice if we had our birthdays all the time? Or we didn't have to wait to buy that toy? Or adults didn't have to work hard and wait to get money? But the Bible tells us in Galatians 5:22 that one of the fruit of the Spirit (the result of spending time with God and having a relationship with Him) is patience. The more we spend time with God, the more we become like Him!

We don't actually have to work really hard to be more like Jesus. Just like when we spend time with our friends, we start to become like them (which is why it is REALLY important to choose good friends), it is the same with Jesus. When we read the Bible and spend time with Him, we become like Him—we produce good things in our life!

Let's do a Word Study to understand better what patience is and what it is not. Circle one synonym and one antonym of the word **patient**.

Synonyms	Antonyms
understanding	wild
calm	stubborn
peaceful	impatient

Flash Card FUN

Make a flashcard with this week's character trait on it and decorate it however you want!

I AM PATIENT

draw it!

This week, you get to draw a picture of you and Jesus to help you remember that God is always with you! Maybe you want to do this on a separate piece of paper, together with your Bible verse to help you remember that He is with you, that He will never leave you, and that you don't have to be afraid!

journal!

Name: _____

Day: 1 2 3 ④

Write this week's key truth.

_____
_____
_____
_____

Write (or have your parent or teacher write) about something you really want to have or do that you need to wait for, and then ask Jesus to help you wait patiently.

_____
_____
_____
_____
_____
_____

NOT ON MY OWN STRENGTH...

Thank You, God, that You are helping me become more patient. Help me learn to wait for Your timing and to trust You more.

I've been learning more about God in my Bible time. I've learned that God is three persons in one, that He is love, that He is good, that He has no beginning or end, and that He is always with me. But even though I know those things, it is really hard to understand! How can someone be three different people but all one person? How can God BE love? How is God there if He was never created? How can He be with me everywhere, and everyone else all at the same time? I have so many questions about God, but Dad told me that our minds can't understand everything about God because He is just bigger than our thoughts.

I guess it's kind of like the bird I saw in the backyard today. It is getting colder now, and Dad said it might even snow soon! The bird didn't look worried. It only understands what God gave it to know: how to eat and take care of its babies and how to fly away when my cat chases it. But it can't understand everything that I can — because God made me bigger and to know more than the bird. So God is bigger and knows more than me and that's okay! One day I'll have LOTS of questions for Him in heaven!

Aliyah

Name: _____

Day: ① 2 3 4

talk about it!

Are there things about God that you don't understand?

Do we have to understand everything about God?

Check it with the Word!
BIBLE

Another important thing to know about God is that He is beyond understanding. That means He is bigger or more than we can ever know. We will never understand everything about God. Some things just get to be a mystery! I love mysteries, don't you? Let's see if we can find this in the Bible. Turn to Job 11:7.

Can you find out the deep things of God? Can you find out the limit of the Almighty?

This verse is Job's friend Zophar speaking to him when he was going through a really hard time. Zophar wasn't really encouraging him. Instead, he was showing him that God was so big and impossible to understand that Job should just accept it. It is really important to understand the context of what we are reading. The context is like the setting, the background story. It tells us where and when the story takes place, who is talking, and helps us begin to understand what the verse might mean. We don't ever want to just pick a verse in the Bible to prove a point without testing it within its context.

KEY TRUTH:

God is beyond understanding

God is beyond understanding
_____
_____
_____
_____
_____

Copywork: Copy your verse for the week on the lines below.

Can you find out the deep things of
God? Can you find out the limit of the
Almighty? (Job 11:7)

Circle all the rhyming words while you read this poem.

God is Bigger

How can God be everywhere
All at the same time?
How can He know everything?
Every secret thought of mine?

How can He love everyone?
No matter what they've done?
How could He have given us
His one and only Son?

How did God make the world
By speaking "Let it be?"
God is so much bigger
Than my mind could ever see.

talk about it!

Remember how we talked about how poems are separated?

Each of the four lines together are called stanzas.

What do these three stanzas teach us about God?

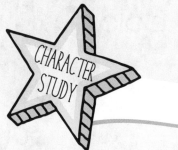

HONEST

Narrate (or tell out loud) to your teacher what it means to be honest. Honest means to tell the truth, even when it's hard. Sometimes when we think of honesty, we think it is the opposite of lying, and it kind of is. But the character trait of honesty is more than that, too! When you are an honest person, you tell the truth, play by the rules, don't exaggerate, admit when you are wrong, and you don't take things that don't belong to you. So it is more than just not lying, isn't it?

To be thought of as an honest person, we learned it is more than just telling the truth when someone asks us a question. Here is a list of synonyms and antonyms for the word honest. Put them in the correct column.

	synonym	antonym
real)		
fair)		
fake)		
lie)		
true)		
false)		

Flash Card FUN
Make a flashcard with this week's character trait on it and decorate it however you want!

57

Name: _____

Day: 1 2 3 ④

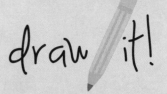
draw it!

This week, we learned what it means to be honest and how God is like a mystery, bigger than we can ever know or learn about or understand! So you have two choices with your drawing today. Circle what you want to draw and then we'll write about it on the next page.

1. Draw a picture of you solving a mystery. Maybe you have binoculars or a magnifying glass.

2. Draw a picture of a time when you told the truth even though it was hard.

journal!

Can you remember your key truth this week? Let's find it and write it here again to help us remember.

_____
....
_____
_____
....
_____

Write two sentences about the picture you drew or what was the most interesting thing you learned this week!

_____
....
_____
_____
....
_____
....
_____

NOT ON MY OWN STRENGTH...

God, I can always trust Your Word, that what You say is true. Help me to be someone who is honest and true, just like You! Thank You that You are making me to be more like You every day, Jesus!

Today my cousins came over! I LOVE my cousins! David is almost the same age as me, and we love to play imaginary games with our big brothers! But after a while, I was feeling kind of left out. The boys were playing and were annoyed with me because I was getting "too crazy," they said. Sometimes I get really excited and am trying really hard to calm down.

The boys were playing outside with pretend swords and the more left out I felt, the more angry I got until someone told mom. She sent me to my room for a while, and I was angry and sad and feeling like no one understood me. Just when I felt the worst, I thought of the Bible verse I had learned where God said, "I will never leave you nor forsake you" (Deuteronomy 31:6). Then our dog came and laid her head on my lap and I didn't feel so alone. God is always with me, and I know that He understands and can help me learn to play better with my friends. I'm going to go outside and say sorry and try to play as a team!

Malakai

Name: _____

Day: ① 2 3 4

talk about it!

Why was Malakai feeling alone?

Do you think God knew that he was lonely?

BIBLE

Check it with the Word!

Did you know that God knows everything? Not just everything that has happened, but everything that WILL happen, and how you are feeling and what you are thinking! God is all-knowing! Open up your Bible to Psalm 139:4:

Even before a word is on my tongue, behold, O LORD, you know it altogether.

This verse shows us that God knows even what we are going to say before we say it. He knows us better than we even know ourselves! So when we are confused or frustrated or feeling lonely, we can ask God for help because He understands everything we are thinking and feeling!

KEY TRUTH:

God knows everything

God knows everything

Name: _____

Day: 1 ②3 4

<u>Copywork:</u> Let's copy our verse to help us remember that God knows everything! As you write it, say the words and think about them to help you write it on your heart, not just your mind!

<u>Even before a word is on my tongue, behold, O LORD, you know it altogether. (Psalm 139:4)</u>

Name: _____

Day: 1 ②③ 3 4

Overview: This hymn is a prayer to God. It is the cry of our hearts to be even closer to Jesus; it is all we want.

JUST A CLOSER WALK WITH THEE

Hymn: verse two	Interpretation:
Thro' this world of toil and snares,	The world has lots of troubles
If I falter, Lord, who cares?	But if I fall down or make a mistake, who cares?
Who with me my burden shares?	Who helps me when I am struggling?
None but Thee, dear Lord, none but Thee.	No one but you, Jesus.

Can you highlight or circle all the rhyming words at the end of the lines?

Read this verse one more time. It means that even though things are hard, God shares our burden. He understands!

talk about it!

You can explore this entire hymn with a line-by-line modern interpretation on page 301.

CHARACTER STUDY

COMPASSIONATE

Do you know what being compassionate means? Being compassionate means you feel deeply for someone who is going through a hard time — whether that be your little sister who hurt herself or kids who are not getting enough food in another country. You don't just care for them, you want to help! Jesus was the best example of showing compassion. He wanted to help and heal everyone of their sicknesses, their suffering, and their pain. The Bible tells us He was moved with compassion (Matthew 9:36) toward the people who came to Him.

Let's look closer at the word **compassionate**. Circle your two favorite synonyms and antonyms from the list below and write them on the chart.

Synonyms:	Antonyms:
merciful, understanding, tender	cold, mean, uncaring

Flash Card FUN
Make a flashcard with this week's character trait on it and decorate it however you want!

WEEK 7: GOD KNOWS EVERYTHING

Name: _____

Day: 1 2 ③ 4

color it!

I am compassionate

Name: _____

Day: 1 2 3 ④

draw it!

Today, we are going to draw a picture of the planets and the stars to help us remember that God knows about everything!

Name: _____

Day: 1 2 3 ④

Write this week's key truth.

_____

_____

_____

_____

Write a prayer thanking God for knowing everything about you!

_____

_____

_____

_____

_____

_____

_____

NOT ON MY OWN STRENGTH . . .

God, You are gracious and show compassion. Give me Your love and compassion for people around me, my friends, my family, and people I meet! Help me to love them the way You do!

journal entry   Aliyah

Week Eight: What Is God's Name?
Day: ①2 3 4

We got a new kitten today! We already have two, but those are outside cats, and this one will be allowed to be in the house! She is so cute and little! She is playful and cuddly, and we are thinking of a really good name for her. Mom is picky about her name because she said names are really important. My parents took a long time to think of my name. They even asked God what my name should be! I asked mom what my name means so we looked it up together and it means "To Rise Up"! I think that is a really cool name to have.

I know God, Jesus, and the Holy Spirit are names of God, but I wonder if God has any other names? I have three names. My first name, middle name, and last name. PLUS I have nicknames that my friends and family call me sometimes. Does God have other names, too?

Aliyah

Name: _____

Day: ① 2 3 4

talk about it!

Do you know your three names (or more if you have more)?

What does your name mean?

Check it with the Word!

Turn in your Bible to Exodus 3:13–14.
We are going to learn a new name of God!

Then Moses said to God, "If I come to the people of Israel and say to them, 'The God of your fathers has sent me to you,' and they ask me, 'What is his name?' what shall I say to them?" God said to Moses, "I AM WHO I AM." And he said, "Say this to the people of Israel: 'I AM has sent me to you.' "

Did you see what God called Himself when Moses asked? Highlight God's name. It's one we wouldn't normally use as a name! Did you find it? One of the ways God describes Himself is I AM. In Hebrew, it is four letters and no vowels, YHWH. But we can't pronounce that, so you will sometimes hear God referred to as Yahweh in some Bible translations or in some books.

Mostly, the names we use for God are: God, Lord, Jesus, Holy Spirit, and Father.

KEY TRUTH:

God is the great I Am

God is the great I Am
_____
_____
_____
_____

<u>Copywork:</u> Let's write these words on the page and in our hearts.

<u>God said to Moses, "I AM WHO I AM." . . . (Exodus 3:14)</u>

The Present by Thomas Cole (1838)

This painting is about days gone by. It shows medieval ruins covered by moss and plants, overgrown over time. Notice how the tower still stands strong. Towers are built to last. The Bible tells us in Proverbs 18:10, "The name of the LORD is a strong tower; the righteous man runs into it and is safe."

LET'S LOOK CLOSER

There are lots of details in this painting. If you have a magnifying glass, that can help you see all the little details that make this painting so special. Point to some areas where the light is and other areas where there is shadow. This gives us a hint about the time of day, probably around when the sun is setting, in the evening. Do you see the shepherd and his goats in the field? The water in the distance? Do you think it is a river? A sea? What time of year do you think it is? See if the color of the leaves on the trees can help give you some clues. Would you like to visit this place? How does it make you feel that God is our strong tower, the great I Am?

Art study

WEEK 8: WHAT IS GOD'S NAME?

72

CHARACTER STUDY

COURAGEOUS

Sometimes when people think of being courageous, they think it means that you aren't afraid, but that isn't always true. Courage is doing what is right even when you are scared. It can mean going through difficult times in our lives and staying strong and brave. It might be a small thing like trying a new food that you think you won't like or something big like telling your mom the truth when you broke something and were afraid she might be angry.

Lets look closer at words that help us understand our word **courageous**.

Synonyms of courageous are:

strong

daring

heroic

Circle your favorite word to help you understand what it means to be courageous.

Antonyms of courageous are:

cowardly

afraid

weak

Flash Card FUN

Make a flashcard with this week's character trait on it and decorate it however you want!

WEEK 8: WHAT IS GOD'S NAME?

color it!

I AM COURAGEOUS

draw it!

Today, we are going to try some word art! You are going to take your favorite name for God and write it in the box below and do some art around it. You could make the words really big or really small. You could draw something behind it or around it!

Name: _____

Day: 1 2 3 ④

Write this week's key truth.

_____
- -
_____
_____
- -
_____

Write about a time when you were courageous.

_____
- -
_____
_____
- -
_____
_____
- -
_____

NOT ON MY OWN STRENGTH . . .

Thank You that fear does not come
from You, Jesus. You want us to be
strong and have courage. Help me
to have more courage, to do what
You want me to!

We have learned SO much about God and who He is, but we don't want to forget it! Each week, you have learned a key truth! Today, we are going to play a game to help us remember what they are.

Pull out pages 319-321 for Quarter 1 and cut out your Key Truth cards. There are lots of ways to help you remember your key truths. You can hop on each card and try to remember what it is or say what it means to you. You can ask a parent to read the first part and see if you can remember the end. You can copy them and decorate them! Think of a fun way you can review your key truths!

If you have been working on your character trait flashcards, this is the week you get to practice them all together! There are so many fun ways to do this! You can practice them on your own by just reading them or you can play a game to make it more fun! You can even play a game with a family member or friend. You can take turns reading the character trait and have the other person say an example, act it out, or explain what it means. Then trade places! You can make another copy of your cards (or have a parent help) and play memory by turning them all over and trying to find matching pairs. You can even put them on the floor in a pattern or build an obstacle course and as you find the cards or land on the cards, say what it is or what it means OR an example of that character trait.

SO many fun ways to review your cards! Choose one or make up your own and see how well you can remember what these character traits look like in action!

Name: _____

Day: 1 ②(circled) 3 4

Highlight, circle, or color the words in the puzzle below. The first one is done for you.

T	Q	U	C	O	N	T	E	N	T	X	U	H	O
M	Y	P	E	R	S	E	V	E	R	E	Q	A	Z
X	H	L	Z	G	P	V	K	K	L	B	M	W	H
K	H	Y	U	L	K	P	Q	O	I	R	O	Y	M
L	H	U	H	O	L	N	F	I	S	L	W	I	A
C	O	U	R	A	G	E	O	U	S	O	W	O	Y
P	A	T	I	E	N	T	H	U	M	B	L	E	Z
K	C	O	M	P	A	S	S	I	O	N	A	T	E
F	E	M	K	R	I	M	J	U	R	J	E	D	K
A	I	D	E	P	E	N	D	A	B	L	E	K	T
H	O	N	E	S	T	V	E	W	O	P	Y	N	E
I	Q	A	C	Y	R	C	N	B	X	O	D	N	O

COMPASSIONATE   DEPENDABLE   PATIENT

CONTENT   HONEST   PERSEVERE

COURAGEOUS   HUMBLE

LET'S CONNECT creatively

WHOLE FAMILY ACTIVITY

To help us reflect on what we have learned about this quarter, we are going to do a creative connection, or artistic, hands-on project! This is optional. If you prefer, you can draw a picture or use playdough or something else to show what you learned.

Gather these items:

· poster board

· markers/pencil crayons

· stickers or whatever you want to decorate the poster

1. Write Who Is God at the top of the poster in big letters (or have a parent or teacher do that).

2. Lay down on the poster board with just your head and upper body and have someone trace you onto the board. Make sure to keep your arms down!

3. Write your key truths onto the poster and the character traits you have learned about to help you show who God is.

4. Decorate it, color it, and put it up on the wall!

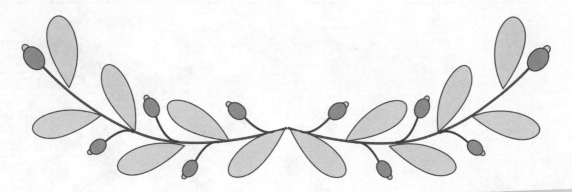

WEEK 9: REVIEW

journal!

What character trait do you think is your strongest?

Which one do you need to work on the most?

What is your favorite thing you learned about God this week?

QUARTER 2:

Who Am I to God?

Journal entry Malakai

Week Ten: Created and Loved

Day: ① 2 3 4

My mom gets lots and lots of mail. Sometimes the mail comes in really big boxes. She loves mail because she usually gets books for our school, but I love it when she gets the mail because sometimes I get to keep the box (when it isn't my brother or sisters' turn). I have used some boxes to make a really cool fort, and I even got to sleep in it last night! Every time I find a new box, I add it to my fort, just like my brother's. I love making new things. Mom says that is called creativity and it is part of who I am because God is really creative too! God created the whole world. He must love creating just as much as I do! I thought God stopped creating after He made the world, but He is always creating, every day, because He makes all the people who are born! Maybe He loves creating even more than I do because I might get tired with that much creative stuff!

Malakai

Day: ① 2 3 4

talk about it!

Do you like making new things?

What are some things you have made lately?

Check it with the Word!

BIBLE

Did you know that God made you? He thought of your eyes and what color they should be and what your personality would be like. Let's open up our Bibles to Psalm 139:13—18 and check what God says about who we are.

For you formed my inward parts; you knitted me together in my mother's womb. I praise you, for I am fearfully and wonderfully made. Wonderful are your works; my soul knows it very well. My frame was not hidden from you, when I was being made in secret, intricately woven in the depths of the earth. Your eyes saw my unformed substance; in your book were written, every one of them, the days that were formed for me, when as yet there was none of them. How precious to me are your thoughts, O God! How vast is the sum of them! If I would count them, they are more than the sand. I awake, and I am still with you.

This week, we are learning that God made us. In Genesis 1:27, when God made the very first people, He said that He made us in His own image! That's kind of how you might look like your dad or your mom!

How many grains of sand do you think there are in the world? More than we can count! Millions! Billions! That is how much God thinks about you! Do you think He loves you very much? I know He does!

KEY TRUTH:

I am created and loved

I am created and loved

Copywork: Think about this week's verse while you write it out below in your neatest handwriting!

I praise you, for I am fearfully and wonderfully made. (Psalm 139:14)

Name: _____

Day: 1 ②③ 3 4

Circle or highlight the rhyming words in the following poem.

God's Masterpiece

Before I was created,
Not even yet a cell,
God thought about my life to be;
My days, He planned them well.

In the secret place He made me:
My heart, my mind, my smile.
He knew who I was meant to be —
His chosen, loved child.

More than the grains of sand
On every water's shore,
My God who made me, loves me,
He thinks about me more.

talk
about it!

Poetry has rhythm, kind of like music. Read it one more time and this time clap out the rhythm of the poem.

Underline your favorite line. Why is that line so special to you?

WEEK 10: CREATED AND LOVED

CHARACTER STUDY

SELF-DISCIPLINED

Being self-disciplined means that you are in control of yourself. You control your feelings, your actions and reactions (like when someone spills something on you!), and you keep going even when you want to stop (like waking up early to read your Bible, even though you're REALLY tired). The Bible talks a lot about self-discipline and self-control. In fact, one of the fruits of the Spirit (the result of spending time with God) is that we are less controlled by our feelings and our environment (what happens to us). Second Timothy 1:7 tells us, "For God gave us a spirit not of fear but of power and love and self-control."

Circle your two favorite synonyms and antonyms of self-discipline and write them on the chart below.

Synonyms:

balance, stability, willpower

Antonyms:

rash, unstable, thoughtless

Flash Card FUN
Make a flashcard with this week's character trait on it and decorate it however you want!

WEEK 10: CREATED AND LOVED

Name:

Day: 1 2 ③ 4

color it!

I AM SELF-DISCIPLINED

Name: _____

Day: 1 2 3 ④

draw it!

Draw a picture of you when you were a baby and some hearts around you to remind you that God made you and loves you (or draw any picture to help you think of what you learned this week).

journal!

What is this week's key truth?

_____

- -

_____

_____

- -

_____

Write your favorite line from the poem on the line below (the one you underlined).

_____

- -

_____

_____

- -

_____

Can you remember an example of self-discipline? Write it below.

_____

- -

_____

_____

- -

_____

NOT ON MY OWN STRENGTH . . .

Jesus, help me to have more
self-control — to think before
I speak or act and not to do
things out of anger or hurt.

WEEK 10: CREATED
AND LOVED

It snowed today! I love the snow! I put on all of my snow gear — my snow pants and mittens and my winter jacket and my boots (which are too small now) — and went outside to see if I could make snowballs! Soon we will be able to go snowmobiling in our backyard and then it will be Christmas! I am so excited! Mom made hot chocolate with mini marshmallows for us, and we all wrote our favorite thing about winter in our tea time. Then my sister spilled her hot chocolate all over the table and all over me! It wasn't very hot anymore, but it made a big mess and I was mad! "JANIAH!" I yelled. "Be more careful!" I had to go upstairs and get changed, and when I came back down, she was crying and trying to clean it up. She's only 4, so she wasn't doing a very good job! I'm 6 already, so I told her I was sorry for getting mad and helped her clean it up. It wasn't really that hard to clean up, after all!

Aliyah

Name: _____

Day: ① 2 3 4

talk about it!

Why was Aliyah mad when Janiah spilled her hot chocolate on her?

Would you be upset if someone did that all over your clothes?

Do you think it hurt Janiah's feelings that Aliyah yelled at her when it was an accident?

What do you think Aliyah should have done instead?

Check it with the Word!

Did you know that we aren't perfect? We make mistakes and we mess up. That's because in the very beginning, when Adam and Eve disobeyed God, sin entered the world. This is called the Fall. Open up your Bible to Romans 3:23:

For all have sinned and fall short of the glory of God.

When we are learning about who we are in God, it is important to understand that none of us are perfect and that everyone makes mistakes. We shouldn't judge other people when they do something wrong because we all fail sometimes!

KEY TRUTH:

No one is perfect

No one is perfect

_____

_____

_____

Name: _____

Day: 1 ②3 4

<u>Copywork:</u> Let's write our verse out today to help us remember that only God is perfect and that we need Him!

For all have sinned and fall short of the glory of God. (Romans 3:23)

Name: _____

Day: 1 ②3 4

Belshazzar's Feast by Rembrandt van Rijn (1606–1669)

Look closely at this picture. This is a painting of a story in the Bible. You can read about the story of Belshazzar in Daniel 5, but I'll tell you a little bit about it here. Belshazzar was a king who took golden goblets from the Temple of God and was using them at a feast and worshiping idols (false gods) while drinking wine from cups from God's house. He made a bad choice, and God wrote a message to him on the wall.

LET'S TAKE A CLOSER LOOK

When you look at this painting, first look at the use of light and shadow. Light and shadow can be used to draw our attention to something, away from something, or to create a mood. There are lots of shadows in this painting. Can you point out where there are shadows and where the light is?

Did you notice how the light is focused on the golden cups, Belshazzar, and the writing on the wall? Everything else falls away into darkness — that is to draw our eyes to the story.

Read the Bible story together with your parent or teacher and study the painting while you listen to see if you notice anything else. All have sinned, and that includes kings and queens.

Art study

WEEK 11: FALLEN AND IMPERFECT

KIND

I bet you know what being kind is, don't you? Kindness is something we practice lots and lots! We show kindness by sharing and listening to people and caring about their thoughts and feelings. When we are being kind, we have to think of other people, not just ourselves. Ephesians 4:32 tells us to, "Be kind to one another, tenderhearted, forgiving one another, as God in Christ forgave you." Sometimes when people annoy or frustrate us or hurt our feelings, it is hard to be kind to them. We want to be just as mean back to them, but God tells us to forgive them and be kind because even though we make mistakes, God loves us!

Synonyms of kind are:

friendly

gentle

thoughtful

Circle your favorite word to help you understand what it means to be kind.

Antonyms of kind are:

cruel

hateful

mean

Flash Card FUN

Make a flashcard with this week's character trait on it and decorate it however you want!

WEEK 11: FALLEN AND IMPERFECT

Name: _____

Day: 1 2 3 ④

draw it!

Draw a picture of you being kind to someone in your family.

journal!

Do you remember your key truth this week? Write it here.

Write a sentence or two about your picture to share how you can be kind.

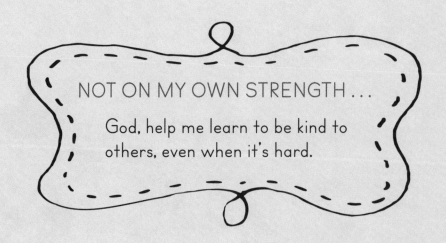

NOT ON MY OWN STRENGTH...

God, help me learn to be kind to others, even when it's hard.

I have wanted a special dinosaur boxed set for as long as I can remember. I love dinosaurs, and I have waited and waited and saved all my money and done extra chores to try to earn it. For my birthday a few weeks ago, Mom and Dad gave me the rest of the money I needed, and we ordered the set online. I waited every day for it to come. I went with my mom to check the mail, and we kept looking on the computer to see where the mail was. FINALLY, it was here! It came in a really big box and was packaged very carefully! I unwrapped it as fast as I could. I didn't even care about the box! It was even bigger than I thought it would be and SO COOL! As soon as I pulled it out and started opening it up, my sister wanted to look at it, too. I was trying really hard to share and let her see, but I also really didn't want her to lose anything or break anything because it was really special to me. I put it in a special bin under my bed where I can keep it safe, and I work on it every day! Now I can't wait to see what it looks like when it is all finished!

Malakai

Name: _____

Day: ① 2 3 4

talk about it!

Why was Malakai so excited about the boxed set?

Did he want just any set or a specific one?

Did you know that God chose you just like you carefully pick out something you really, really want? God was thinking about you even before you were made! He was dreaming about you and planning what you would be like and looking forward to the day you would be born. God doesn't just accept us when we have a relationship with Him — the Bible says He chose us.

BIBLE — Check it with the Word!

Open up your Bible to John 15:16:

You did not choose me, but I chose you and appointed you that you should go and bear fruit and that your fruit should abide, so that whatever you ask the Father in my name, he may give it to you.

Who do you think is talking in this verse? Remember how we talked about context —seeing the whole picture, not just a part? If we look at this whole passage of the Bible, this is Jesus talking. Underline or highlight the part that says, "I chose you." Pray together with your parent or teacher, or all by yourself, and thank Jesus that He chose you.

KEY TRUTH:

God chose me

God chose me

Copywork: Write the following verse and think about what it means that God chose you. How wonderful that is!

You did not choose me, but I chose you. (John 15:16)

Overview: This hymn is about being chosen for God's plans — that you were thought of before the world was even made, and God wanted you in His family.

DO YOU KNOW THAT YOU WERE CHOSEN

Hymn: verse one	Interpretation:
Do you know that you were chosen	God chose you!
Long before the world began	Before He even made the world!
That by God you were selected	He thought of you!
And appointed for His plan?	And had a plan for you!
Something in your inmost being	Something deep inside you
Tells you this is surely true;	knows this is true

talk about it!

Can you find your key truth, that you are chosen, in this verse of the hymn? Highlight it or underline it. This hymn was written by Charles Crozat Converse. Read it through with a parent or teacher and circle all the rhyming words.

Now go listen to it and see what it sounds like when it is put to music!

You can explore this entire hymn with a line-by-line modern interpretation on pages 303-304.

CHARACTER STUDY

OPTIMISTIC

Optimistic is just a big word that means being positive, hoping for or thinking of good things instead of always thinking about what could go wrong. It is kind of like waking up in the morning and either thinking, "This is going to be a GREAT day!" or waking up in a bad mood and thinking, "This day is terrible." How you choose to view things that happen determines your attitude. The Bible tells us in Philippians 4:13, "I can do all things through Christ who strengthens me." Next time you face something that looks hard, like doing the dishes or cleaning your room, remind yourself of that verse and find the good in it instead of thinking of the hard parts!

☐☐☐☐☐☐☐☐☐☐

Write these synonyms and antonyms for optimistic in the correct column of the chart below.

sad, hopeful, cheerful, unhappy, depressed, positive

Synonyms:	Antonyms:

Flash Card FUN

Make a flashcard with this week's character trait on it and decorate it however you want!

WEEK 12: CHOSEN

Name:

Day: 1 2 ③ 4

color it!

I AM OPTIMISTIC

Name: _____

Day: 1 2 3 ④

Draw a picture of how you show your optimism or how you would like to show it more!

WEEK 12: CHOSEN

Name: _____

Day: 1 2 3 ④

Can you remember your key truth?

_____
_ _ _ _ _ _ _ _ _ _ _ _ _ _ _ _ _ _ _ _
_____
_____
_ _ _ _ _ _ _ _ _ _ _ _ _ _ _ _ _ _ _ _
_____

Write your favorite line of our hymn this week.

_____
_ _ _ _ _ _ _ _ _ _ _ _ _ _ _ _ _ _ _ _
_____
_____
_ _ _ _ _ _ _ _ _ _ _ _ _ _ _ _ _ _ _ _
_____
_____
_ _ _ _ _ _ _ _ _ _ _ _ _ _ _ _ _ _ _ _
_____

NOT ON MY OWN STRENGTH...

God, help me to be more optimistic, to see the good things and not just the bad things. Thank You that all my hope comes from You!

Today I had a hard day. I was kind of grumpy when I woke up and the day just got worse and worse. I was annoyed at my brothers, and I yelled at my sister, and I cried when it was time for school. Mommy kept talking to me about my attitude and that I had to change it, but I just couldn't! Even when I tried, I kept on getting upset and making mistakes. Finally, Mom took me to my room and talked to me. She told me that I had to have a nap. I hate naps! I cried even harder, but she said that it wasn't a punishment, it was to help me. She said that even grownups get really tired sometimes, and when we are so, so tired, it gets harder and harder to have self-control, like being patient and kind and not getting upset so easily or overwhelmed.

I didn't like it, but I fell asleep pretty fast and when I woke up, I felt so much better! Things didn't bother me so much, and I wasn't as angry and sad. I guess Mom was right! Even though I didn't know it, I was really tired!

Aliyah

Name: _____

Day: ① 2 3 4

talk about it!

Do you ever wake up grumpy?

Even though Aliyah didn't know how to change her attitude, her mom knew how to help her, didn't she?

How did her mom fix Aliyah's problem?

Do you know that we have a problem, too? Our problem is that we have all sinned. We are not perfect. Heaven is a beautiful, perfect place, and none of us deserve to be there. But God loves us SO much that He sent His Son, Jesus, to die for our sins. Jesus took the punishment for our sin so that we could go to heaven and be saved!

Check it with the Word!

BIBLE

Open up your Bible to John 3:16:

For God so loved the world, that he gave his only Son, that whoever believes in him should not perish but have eternal life.

God had a plan to save us when we couldn't do anything to earn it. We are kind of like Aliyah — we know we should do what is right, but we make mistakes even when we try hard! God fixed the problem. He didn't make us perfect, but Jesus takes away our sin so that we can have the free gift of salvation (that means going to heaven)! All we have to do is ask Him, and no matter what bad things we have done, Jesus washes us clean and saves us from our sin!

KEY TRUTH:

I am saved by Jesus

I am saved by Jesus

Name: _____

Day: 1 ②3 4

<u>Copywork:</u> Do you remember what God's plan to save us from our sin was? He sent His son! Copy this part of the verse and think about how good God is.

Whoever believes in him should not perish but have eternal life. (John 3:16)

Name: _____

Day: 1 ②3 4

Why did Jesus die on the Cross? Read this poem and share the answer.

The Great Plan

Sometimes I fall.
I do bad things.
But God loves me,
His grace He brings.

He has a gift
For anyone
Who will believe
His only Son.

He sent His Son
To die for me
So I could live
Eternally.

I thank You, God
For choosing me
In your great plan
To set me free,

talk about it!

What does it mean to live eternally? It means that we will go to heaven when we die and live there forever and ever!

WEEK 13: SAVED

CHARACTER STUDY

THANKFUL

Being thankful means you have a grateful heart. Why do you think it is important to be thankful? Did you know that thankfulness is part of the recipe for joy and contentment? When we are thankful for all the things God gives us, it helps us to be more joyful and to see God's goodness all around us! We can be grateful for big things like our family, but also for little things — like your bed and pillow or even the new little flowers outside. First Thessalonians 5:18 tells us to give thanks in all circumstances. That means even the hard ones!

Circle your favorite 2 synonyms.

grateful

pleased

praise

THANKFUL

selfish

unhappy

rude

Flash Card FUN

Make a flashcard with this week's character trait on it and decorate it however you want!

WEEK 13: SAVED

I AM THANKFUL

Name: _____

Day: 1 2 3 ④

draw it!

Draw a picture of the Cross to help you remember that Jesus died for you.

WEEK 13: SAVED

journal!

Can you remember our key truth for the week?

_____
_____
_____
_____

Talk about or write out some of the things you are thankful for today.

_____
_____
_____
_____
_____

NOT ON MY OWN STRENGTH . . .

God, help me to have a grateful heart for everything you have given me.

WEEK 13: REDEEMED
AND SAVED

Today I went all by myself to a new friend's house and had so much fun! His name is Thomas. He had so many cool toys, even a remote control helicopter! We played all afternoon until his mom called us into the kitchen for fresh cookies and milk, my favorite! The cookies were still warm and gooey, and she let us have 3 each (my mom only lets us have 2)! It was the best day ever! Thomas told me that he was adopted. That is why his skin is a different color than his mom's. He showed me a map on the wall of where he was from in Africa and how he wants to go there to visit one day. It made me think about how God adopted us into HIS family. We aren't just children of our parents, we are also children of God — kind of like having two families! That's the same as Thomas!

Malakai

Name: _____

Day: ① 2 3 4

talk about it!

Do you know what adopted means? It means to be chosen to be in a relationship, like to be someone's son or daughter or brother or sister.

Did you know that we are adopted into God's family? When He chose us, and when we believe in Him, we become His children!

Check it with the Word!

The Bible tells us in Ephesians 1:5

He predestined us for adoption to himself as sons through Jesus Christ, according to the purpose of his will.

Predestined is a really big word that means He chose us before we were even born, to be His sons and daughters, (to adopt us) through Jesus Christ. That was the great big plan! Even though we can never be perfect, we have a way to be with God in heaven because of what Jesus did for us on the Cross!

Pretty cool, huh?

KEY TRUTH:

I am adopted

I am adopted

WEEK 14: ADOPTED

116

<u>Copywork:</u> Copy the verse and think about how wonderful it is to be adopted by God.

<u>He predestined us for adoption to</u>
<u>himself as sons through Jesus Christ</u>
<u>... (Ephesians 1:5)</u>

Fisherman's Family by Winslow Homer (1881)

Like all paintings, this picture is telling us a story. There are all sorts of clues in the colors, the details, the landscape, and even the title of the painting. This is called Fisherman's Family, which tells us it is the picture of a family, possibly watching their fisherman leave for the open ocean or return.

LET'S LOOK CLOSER

If you have a magnifying glass, pull it out and let's look a little closer. You'll notice that there are fewer little details than some of the other paintings we have looked at. Do you see very defined strokes of the paintbrush? Not on this one! The reason is the medium, or what was used. Rather than using oil paint, this is watercolor. Watercolor is a type of paint that blends with water and is much less intricate or detailed than some other forms of painting. Notice the steam coming from the boat in the horizon. How do the girls look like they are feeling as they look off at the water? The artist is showing us that they are maybe a little bit lonely or sad, or wishing they were all together. That is the love of a family!

Art study

WEEK 14: ADOPTED

118

PEACEFUL

Peaceful is a word that can mean a few different things. You can be peaceful in your life by being calm and not being stressed or anxious. Peace in relationships means to have no fighting. It can even mean no war or agreeing to end war. When we are talking about the character trait of being peaceful, it means that you don't fight with people. Also, you trust God and don't worry about what will happen because you know He is always looking out for you. The Bible tells us that God's peace will guard our hearts and minds (Philippians 4:7).

→→→→→→→→→→→→→→→→→→→→→→→→→→→→→→→→→→→

Copy two of your favorite synonyms and antonyms for **peaceful** and write them in the right column.

Synonym		Antonym	
harmony)		fighting)	
calm)		worried)	
rest)		angry)	

Flash Card FUN
Make a flashcard with this week's character trait on it and decorate it however you want!

WEEK 14: ADOPTED

Name:

Day: 1 2 ③ 4

color it!

I AM
PEACEFUL

Draw a picture of your family to help you remember that you are a part of God's family.

Name: _____

Day: 1 2 3 ④

Can you remember our key truth for the week?

·····················

·····················

Write out a prayer thanking God for adopting you into His family.

·····················

·····················

·····················

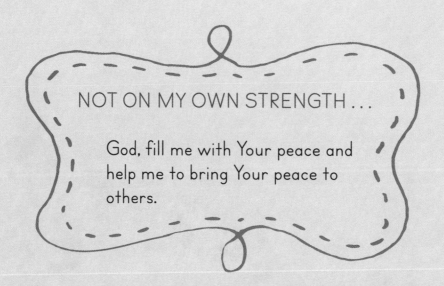

NOT ON MY OWN STRENGTH...

God, fill me with Your peace and
help me to bring Your peace to
others.

It is almost Christmas! The house is all decorated and the Christmas music is playing all the time! Yesterday we baked cookies instead of doing school. I can hardly wait for Christmas to be here! I was so excited today that I was dancing to the music in the living room and when I turned around, Janiah was dancing, too. She was copying me! I laughed and told her to stop, but everything I did, she tried to do, too! Mom said it is because she thinks I am pretty special and wants to be like me. I guess that is okay then. We danced together, and I was laughing so much because she kept on copying me!

Sometimes I copy my mom, too. I pretend that I have a computer or I am on the phone or play imaginary games about cleaning or having kids. Does everyone copy someone they think is special? I am going to ask my sister if she copies anyone.

Aliyah

Name: _____

Day: ① 2 3 4

talk about it!

Why was Janiah copying her sister?

Do you ever copy anyone or try to be like them?

Check it with the Word!

BIBLE

Open up your Bible to Ephesians 5:1−2 and let's read together:

Therefore be imitators of God, as beloved children. And walk in love, as Christ loved us and gave himself up for us, a fragrant offering and sacrifice to God.

The Bible tells us to be imitators of God. Imitate means to copy! So we are supposed to copy God, to love others just like Jesus loved us! The very best example for us to follow and be like is Jesus.

KEY TRUTH:

I am an imitator of God

I am an imitator of God

_____

_____

_____

_____

Copywork: As you copy out this verse, think about how you can show God's love.

Therefore be imitators of God, as beloved children. (Ephesians 5:1)

Overview: This song is about giving God our hands and our feet, our voices and our money, our time and our love, and asking God to use it all for what He wants.

Listen to your parent or teacher read the song, then circle or highlight the rhyming words together.

TAKE MY LIFE AND LET IT BE

Hymn: verse three		Interpretation:
Take my voice and let me sing		I give You my voice, let me sing
Always only for my King		For You, my King (God)
Take my lips, and let them be		I give You my lips, let my mouth be
Filled with messages from Thee		Filled with Your words
Filled with messages from Thee.		Filled with Your words

What are some talents people have?

What are some ways you can give your gifts and talents to God?

talk about it!

You can explore this entire hymn with a line-by-line modern interpretation on pages 305-306.

WEEK 15: IMITATOR OF CHRIST

CHARACTER STUDY

RESPECTFUL

Name: _____

Day: 1 2 ③ 4

Respectful means to value or care about someone else — to listen to them, to treat them as you want to be treated. We can respect our mom and dad by obeying them. This shows them that we care about what they say. We can respect our brothers and sisters and friends by not calling them names because we care about their feelings. We can show respect by being quiet in a library so that other people can read. Every time we think about other people and how they might be feeling and treat them kindly, we are being respectful.

From the list below, circle two of your favorite synonyms and antonyms for respectful.

Synonyms

caring

kind

honor

Antonyms

rude

mean

not kind

Flash Card FUN

Make a flashcard with this week's character trait on it and decorate it however you want!

127

Name: _____

Day: 1 2 ③ 4

color it!

I AM
RESPECTFUL

Day: 1 2 3 ④

draw it!

Can you draw a picture of shoes? When you draw a picture of shoes, it can help you think of walking with God and being more like Him!

WEEK 15: IMITATOR
OF CHRIST

journal!

Can you remember our key truth for the week?
(Look back for the key if you can't remember.):

_____
_____
_____
_____

Write one way you can show respect to someone in your family.

_____
_____
_____
_____
_____

NOT ON MY OWN STRENGTH . . .

God help me to be more and more like
you. Teach me more about who you are
and help me remember to spend time
with you so that you can change me into
who you want me to be.

WEEK 15: IMITATOR
OF CHRIST

Today Dad was working outside in the shed. It is SO cold here and there is lots and lots of snow! So much snow, that sometimes it is hard to walk. I have to jump in the holes that dad leaves with his big boots! Dad was working on plugging in all the cars so the engines didn't freeze because it's supposed to get even colder! Sometimes he asks me to help him. He gives me important jobs. I like it when I work together with dad! When he goes away for work, then I have even more important jobs. He always talks to me and my brother and tells us that we have to take care of our sisters and our mom and do the jobs that he normally does, like taking out the garbage and helping mom lift heavy things. Sometimes people think I'm small, but I'm really strong and I can even carry the water bottles for mom all by myself! It's okay that I have important jobs because I know that my family needs me!

Malakai

Name: _____

Day: ① 2 3 4

Just like Malakai has jobs to do in his house, we have jobs to do for God! God created us and chose us, and He calls us to do His work, too! Do you know what your job is for Jesus?

God will give you lots of different jobs in your life, but one of your jobs is to tell other people about Him! Before Jesus went up to heaven, He even told His disciples to go and make disciples (followers of Jesus) of all nations!

Check it with the Word!
BIBLE

Open up your Bible to Matthew 28:19—20 and let's read:

Go therefore and make disciples of all nations, baptizing them in the name of the Father and of the Son and of the Holy Spirit, teaching them to observe all that I have commanded you. And behold, I am with you always, to the end of the age.

Part of who you are as a Christian is a follower of Christ. You get to tell other people about Him and share His love with everyone you meet! THAT is your calling! You can share God's love with your mom when she is having a hard day, with your brother (even when he is being mean), and with your friends! When you spend time with God, He fills you with His love and joy and peace and patience, and you spill out those things onto other people. God can use you every day, right in your family, right in your home!

KEY TRUTH:

I am called

I am called

_____

_____

_____

_____

_____

Copywork: Let's copy the words of Matthew 28:19.

Make disciples of all nations.
(Matthew 28:19)

Name: _____

Day: 1 (2) 3 4

Read this poem and see some simple ways God can use you to bless others today.

I have a calling

I have a calling,
A job to do —
To share God's love
And speak His truth.

God can use me
Everyday
If I listen
To the words He says.

He can use my smile,
He can use my hands,
He can use my words,
He can use my plans.

God, I give you
This brand new day.
Help me hear
Your will, Your way.

talk about it!

LET'S TALK ABOUT IT!

Let's pray and ask God what He wants us to do today.

How do you think you can show God's love today?

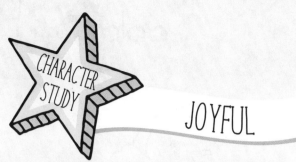

CHARACTER STUDY

JOYFUL

Did you know that joy and happiness are not the same thing? Sometimes when we think of joy, we think it means the same thing, but happiness is just a feeling, and feelings can come and go away really fast — like when you feel happy you got a toy but then really angry just one second later when someone tries to play with it. Being joyful is not a feeling, it is a fruit of the Spirit (that means something that comes from spending time with God). We can't feel it on our own, we get it from God! It is a gift from Him! The Bible even tells us that the joy of the Lord will be our strength (Nehemiah 8:10).

Let's learn more about what being joyful means by looking at some similar words (synonyms) and opposite words (antonyms). Put these words in the correct column.

sad, glad, cheerful, troubled, delighted, sorrowful

Synonyms:

Antonyms:

Flash Card FUN
Make a flashcard with this week's character trait on it and decorate it however you want!

WEEK 16: CALLED

draw it!

Can you draw a picture of a job that you have to do in your home? Maybe it is a chore or cleaning your room. This can help you remember that God has a special job for you, too, and being used by Him can even help fill us with His joy!

WEEK 16: CALLED

journal!

Can you remember our key truth for the week?
(Look back for the key if you can't remember.):

_____
- -
_____
_____
- -
_____

Write or narrate to your teacher something you can do today to show God's love.

_____
- -
_____
_____
- -
_____
_____
- -
_____

NOT ON MY OWN STRENGTH . . .

God, thank You that joy comes
from You! I ask You to fill me
with Your joy today and teach me
more about it!

Today we were writing for our tea time, and mom told us to write about ourselves — who we are! I like writing about that because I know lots about me! I am silly and goofy and funny and happy, and I have lots of friends and I like school and I am good at writing. I had a whole list of things! Sometimes when I think about all those things, it makes me wonder about God. He put all those things inside me! He made me just the way I am! I wonder if God sees different things in me than I do? Who does He think I am?

Aliyah

talk
about it!

What are some things you like about yourself?
Do you think God has a list about you, too?

Name: _____

Day: ① 2 3 4

The Bible has all sorts of verses that help us know who He says we are, and those are really important to know when we feel left out or when we feel that people don't like us, or when we feel bad that we made a mistake. Highlight the key word or words in each verse below that talk about who we are in God. The first one is done for you!

Check it with the Word!

BIBLE

You are loved (John 3:16)

You are free from sin (Romans 8:2)

You are holy and blameless (Ephesians 1:4)

You have the Spirit of God (1 John 4:4)

You are chosen by God (1 Peter 2:9)

You are God's workmanship (Ephesians 2:10)

You are forgiven (Ephesians 1:7)

You are not ruled by fear (2 Timothy 1:7)

You are strong (Colossians 1:11)

You have everything you need (2 Timothy 3:16–17)

You can do all things (Philippians 4:13)

You are fearfully and wonderfully made (Psalm 139:14)

You are never alone, He is always with you (Deuteronomy 31:6)

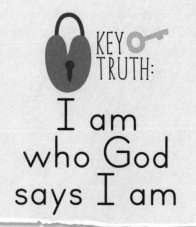

KEY TRUTH:

I am who God says I am

I am who God says I am

Copywork: Have your parent or teacher underline a section or all of the reference below for you to copy.

For we are his workmanship, created
in Christ Jesus for good works, . . .
(Ephesians 2:10)

The Banjo Lesson by Henry Ossawa Tanner (1893)

This is a painting of an elderly man teaching a little boy how to play the banjo. The picture can help you think of God as your teacher, who gives good gifts, and you are His child. It can also help you remember God as someone who is a master musician, a master creator. A master is someone who is really, really good at something. God is really, really good at creating, and He says that you are His workmanship!

LET'S LOOK CLOSER

The medium of this painting is oil on canvas. Notice the broad strokes rather than fine details in the painting. The hair seems almost to disappear. Remember how artists use light and detail to draw our attention to what they want to show us? The center of the painting and more of the light shines on the boy than on the man. Point to a few different things you notice in the painting. What colors are used? Where is the light? Where are the shadows?

Art study

CHARACTER STUDY

COOPERATIVE

What do you think it means to be cooperative? It means to work well together with others! Have you ever had a fight while you were playing a game? Maybe it's because you or someone else wanted to change the rules or maybe they wanted to choose all the games you would play. Working together with other people isn't easy because it means that we may have to not do what we want and instead do what someone else wants. That's hard! But God tells us in Philippians 2:4 that we should not just think about what we want, but also what other people want.

Let's learn more about what cooperative means by looking at some similar words (synonyms) and opposite words (antonyms). Circle your favorite two.

Synonyms	Antonyms
working together	unhelpful
united	separate
team	not supporting

Flash Card FUN

Make a flashcard with this week's character trait on it and decorate it however you want!

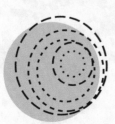

Name: _____
Day: 1 2 ③ 4

color it!

I AM COOPERATIVE

Name: _____

draw it!

Draw a picture of you with big muscles to show you are strong or a picture of you with some friends to remind you that you are never alone or even you inside of a heart to show that you are loved! Go back over the list and see if you can draw one of those things in a picture!

journal!

Name: _____

Day: 1 2 3 ④

Can you remember our key truth for the week?
(Look back for the key if you can't remember.):

_____
- -
_____
_____
- -
_____

Write or narrate to your teacher one way you can cooperate today.

_____
- -
_____
_____
- -
_____
_____
- -
_____

NOT ON MY OWN STRENGTH...

God, help me learn how to work
well with others — how to think of
what other people want and how
they are feeling, not just myself. I
want to be more like You.

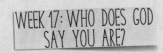

We have learned SO much about who I am to God, but we don't want to forget it! Each week, you have learned a key truth! Today, we are going to play a game to help us remember what they are.

Pull out pages 323-325 for Quarter 2 and cut out your Key Truth cards. There are lots of ways to help you remember your key truths. You can hop on each card and try to remember what it is or say what it means to you. You can ask a parent to read the first part and see if you can remember the end. You can copy them out and you can decorate them! Think of a fun way you can review your key truths!

If you have been working on your character trait flashcards, this is the week you get to practice them all together! There are so many fun ways to do this! You can practice them on your own by just reading them through or you can play a game to make it more fun! You can even play a game with a family member or friend. You can take turns reading the character trait and have the other person say an example, act it out, or explain what it means. Then trade places! You can make another copy of your cards (or have a parent help) and play memory by turning them all over and trying to find matching pairs. You can even put them on the floor in a pattern or build an obstacle course and as you find the cards or land on the cards, say what it is or what it means OR an example of that character trait.

SO many fun ways to review your cards! Choose one or make up your own and see how well you can remember what these character traits look like in action!

Name: _____

Day: 1 ②③ 3 4

Highlight, circle, or color the words in the puzzle below.

W	Q	N	H	Y	M	K	J	C	C	M	P	A	M
Q	E	X	C	H	P	E	A	C	E	F	U	L	J
W	D	I	S	C	I	P	L	I	N	E	D	J	A
X	V	H	R	V	J	O	Y	F	U	L	Y	F	I
I	N	C	O	O	P	E	R	A	T	I	V	E	H
I	R	E	S	P	E	C	T	F	U	L	M	S	H
K	C	O	P	T	I	M	I	S	T	I	C	I	A
N	T	H	R	Z	O	V	A	X	F	U	O	G	Z
K	I	G	U	J	P	Y	Y	S	O	X	U	X	B
K	H	L	B	I	D	H	N	Y	W	P	N	D	J
A	H	H	P	G	Y	T	H	A	N	K	F	U	L
S	A	P	N	O	I	D	K	I	N	D	N	B	V

COOPERATIVE   JOYFUL   PEACEFUL

DISCIPLINED   KIND   RESPECTFUL

THANKFUL   OPTIMISTIC

WEEK 18: REVIEW

148

To help us reflect on what we have learned about this quarter we are going to do a creative connection, or artistic, hands-on project! This is optional. If you prefer, you can draw a picture or use playdough or something to show what you learned.

Supplies needed:

- paint (any kind you have around)

- any paper

- paintbrushes

- marker or pen

LET'S CONNECT

creatively

WHOLE FAMILY ACTIVITY

Instructions: Today we are going to make a rainbow! Do you know how many colors are in the rainbow? Seven! Red, orange, yellow, green, blue, indigo, and violet. We are going to paint the rainbow on our paper, and in each color (once the paint dries) we will write out one of your key truths (the first 7 in this quarter):

I am created and loved.

No one is perfect.

God chose me.

God saved me.

I am adopted.

I am an imitator of God.

I am called.

1. Have a parent or teacher use a pencil to sketch out a rainbow on the paper first if that will help.

2. Fill in each section with the colors of the rainbow. Start at the top with red and fill in the colors down the page.

3. Once your painting has dried, write a word or your entire key truth on each section.

WEEK 18: REVIEW

journal!

Name:

Day: 1 2 3 ④

What do you think is your strongest character trait?

Which one do you need to work on the most?

What is your favorite thing you learned about God this week?

WEEK 18: REVIEW

150

QUARTER 3:

Walking the Walk

Some days I am shy. When I go somewhere new, or when there are lots of people, I don't like it when people ask me questions and everyone is watching me. I feel embarrassed. This week in Sunday school, Mrs. Drycke asked me to pray out loud for the week, and my face felt really hot and my heart was beating really fast. "Please help us to have a good week, God. Amen," I quickly said.

Later, at home, I asked mom why some people are better at praying than other people. She told me it takes practice. Maybe I need to practice praying out loud more and then it won't feel so hard. But sometimes, I just don't know what to say.

Malakai

talk about it!

Why do you think Malakai's face felt hot and his heart was beating fast?

Do you ever feel embarrassed or shy to pray out loud?

Jesus taught us how to pray by giving us a model. That means He gave us an example that we can copy and learn from!

Day: ① 2 3 4

Open up your Bible to Matthew 6:9-13. We call this The Lord's Prayer. When we look at this prayer, it teaches us that we should praise God for who He is, thank Him, ask Him to do what He wants (not just what we want), ask Him to provide for what we need, and ask Him to forgive us and help us to do what is right. Do you think we can practice? Remember, the more you pray, the easier it gets! See if you can pray and try to remember some of the things that we learned in The Lord's Prayer today!

These verses have some confusing words, but we'll help you know what they mean.

Check it with the Word!
BIBLE

Our Father in heaven, hallowed be your name.
(You are God, our heavenly Father, you are holy/sacred/worthy of respect)

Your kingdom come, your will be done, on earth as it is in heaven
(Come and have your way, whatever you want)

Give us this day our daily bread
(Give me what I need today)

And forgive us our debts, as we also have forgiven our debtors.
(forgive me as I forgive other people)

And lead us not into temptation
(help me to not be tempted or want to do wrong)

But deliver us from evil
(save me from bad, scary, or wrong things)

KEY TRUTH:

I can talk to God

I can talk to God

Copywork: Write these words on your heart as well as on the page.

Our Father in heaven, hallowed be
your name. (Matthew 6:9)

Read the verse and then circle or highlight the rhyming words.

SWEET HOUR OF PRAYER

Hymn: verse one		Interpretation:
Sweet hour of prayer! Sweet hour of prayer!		Sweet hour of prayer Sweet hour of prayer
That calls me from a world of care,		That calls me from my worries
And bids me at my Father's throne		And says "Come to God's throne"
Make all my wants and wishes known.		And tell Him what you want
In seasons of distress and grief,		In hard times, in sad times
My soul has often found relief,		My soul finds rest
And oft escaped the tempter's snare,		I have often escaped temptation
By thy return, sweet hour of prayer!		Through prayer

talk
about it!

This song is all about prayer. Praying to God helps us not be worried about what is happenings. How often do you pray? How can prayer help us each day?

You can explore this entire hymn with a line-by-line modern interpretation on pages 309-310.

CHARACTER STUDY

ADAPTABLE

Adaptable means to be able to change or try new things, not just doing things the way they have always been. Like when you are playing a game and your friend says, "Let's do it this way instead!" Maybe you really don't want to change the game, but you try it anyway. That is being adaptable . . . willing to change. It kind of means it doesn't always have to be your way. James 3:17 tells us that God's wisdom is, "open to reason." That means we are willing to listen to other good ideas.

Let's learn more about what adaptable means by looking at some similar words (synonyms) and opposite words (antonyms). Write these words in the correct column of the chart below.

stubborn, easy-going, rigid, flexible, understanding, resistant

Synonyms:	Antonyms:

Flash Card FUN

Make a flashcard with this week's character trait on it and decorate it however you want!

157

I AM
ADAPTABLE

draw it!

Draw a picture of something to help you remember to pray. Maybe it is you talking to God, or hands folded together, or even a speech bubble like the one shown to help us think about praying.

WEEK 19: HOW TO PRAY

journal!

Name: _____

Day: 1 2 3 ④

Can you remember our key truth for the week?

_____
_____
_____
_____

Write or narrate to your teacher a prayer to God.

_____
_____
_____
_____
_____

NOT ON MY OWN STRENGTH...

Thank You, God, that You give good gifts when we ask for them. Give me wisdom to know when to listen, and help me to be open to other people's ideas too!

I am SO excited because today my mom got a package in the mail and she said it was for me! My mom said that when we learn how to read, we get our very own Bible. I am in first grade and know how to read lots and lots of words! I opened up the box carefully, and inside was a beautiful Bible, just for me! It even had my name on the front cover! I was so happy I hugged my mom, and now I have been trying to read in it all day, but it has some really big words. There are words everywhere! Some are at the top of the pages. There are numbers that are big and numbers that are small. Mom said it is time for me to learn how to read my Bible. When school started, I was working on learning the books of the Bible. Mom showed me how the chapters are big and the verses are smaller, and where the New Testament is and the Old. There is lots to know about the Bible!

Aliyah

Name: _____

Day: ① 2 3 4

talk about it!

Can you remember some of the books of the Bible?

There are lots of books in the Bible, but they are organized into two sections: the Old Testament and the New Testament. The Old Testament starts in the very beginning (before the earth was even made) and takes us to before Jesus was born. The New Testament starts with Jesus coming to earth and has all the books that come after that. They show us the new way we get to live because of Jesus and what He did for us!

Why do you think Aliyah was excited to get her own Bible?

BIBLE Check it with the Word!

It is very important to learn how to read the Bible, how to find things in the Bible, and how to understand what it says. Hebrews 4:12 tells us that:

The Word of God is alive and active.

Psalm 119:105 tells us that:

God's Word is a lamp to my feet and a light to my path.

Which one do you think is the most interesting? Choose one of those references to look up with your teacher. The more you use your Bible, the easier it will be to find what you are looking for. A good idea is that when you are reading and something makes you think "wow!" then write down the verse you found it in.

KEY TRUTH:

God's Word is powerful

God's Word is powerful

_____

_____

_____

_____

<u>Copywork:</u> Today, we are going to write out one of the reasons that it is important to know how to read our Bible. See if you can turn to Psalm 119 and think about the words while you write them.

Your word is a lamp to my feet and a light to my path. (Psalm 119:105)

Circle or highlight the rhyming words.

Poetry

I can read my Bible

I can read my Bible,
I know where I can look
To find a verse that helps me.
It is a special book.

I can read my Bible
Each and every day,
To help me make right choices
To show my feet the way.

I can read my Bible.
God's words are always true.
They strengthen and renew me
And give me comfort too.

I can read my Bible,
Even when it's hard.
I practice spending time with God
To help me be on guard.

talk about it!

Can you find the rhythm in this poem? Read it one more time and this time clap out the rhythm.

Underline your favorite line.

Circle your favorite stanza, or section. Why is it your favorite?

TRUSTWORTHY

To be trustworthy is kind of like what we learned about being dependable. It means that people can trust you, rely on you, depend on you. Trust is something that must be earned. People who don't know you won't trust you because they don't know you! You have to get to know people first. They say they will give you something and they do; they say they will help and they will; they say they will be there and they are. Every time someone does something they say they will, it begins to build trust.

We trust people in our family because we know them and because even though they sometimes let us down, they love us. Trust and love and respect go together. When you love someone, you care about them. When you care about what they think and feel, you respect them, and they can trust you. God is the most trustworthy person of all. He is the only one who will never let us down. Psalm 37:5 tells us to trust in God and He will act.

Let's learn more about what trustworthy means by looking at some similar words (synonyms) and opposite words (antonyms). Circle your favorite two.

dependable   **TRUSTWORTHY**   dishonest

honest   lying

truthful   uncertain

Flash Card FUN
Make a flashcard with this week's character trait on it and decorate it however you want!

WEEK 20: HOW TO USE YOUR BIBLE

Name: _____

Day: 1 2 3 ④

draw it!

Draw a picture of the Bible to help you remember to read God's Word. Maybe it is a picture of you reading the Bible, or just the Bible on its own, or the Bible and a sword.

WEEK 20: HOW TO USE YOUR BIBLE

journal!

Can you remember our key truth for the week?

_____

_____

_____

Write or narrate to your teacher about someone you trust and why.

_____

_____

_____

_____

NOT ON MY OWN STRENGTH...

Thank You, Lord, that I can trust
You. Teach me how to be more
trustworthy; help me to do what I
say I will.

Journal entry *Malakai*

Week Twenty-one: What Is Worship?
Day: ① 2 3 4

Mom and Dad are practicing this week for church on Sunday. They lead worship sometimes and sing together, then all us kids have to be really good and help take care of our brothers and sisters so they don't go to Mom and Dad. I love it when Mom and Dad practice because I have a cajon (it's a big box I sit on and drum) and am learning how to find the rhythm and play with them! One day, I want to be a drummer!

When Mom and Dad worship God, they sometimes close their eyes. Mom told me that worship means to praise God, to lift His name up, to celebrate who He is. She says sometimes closing her eyes helps her concentrate on the words and really mean them, not just sing the tune.

Does worship only mean singing?

Malakai

Name: _____

Day: ① 2 3 4

talk about it!

Worship doesn't just mean singing, it means to love God very, very much and respond to our love for Him. Being thankful for what He has given us, doing something for Him, or showing our love for Him are all ways we can worship. Circle the things that you could do while thinking about God and that could be acts of worship:

DANCING   CLEANING YOUR ROOM

SHARING A TOY   PRAYING

SINGING   DOING YOUR SCHOOL WORK

Did you circle all of them? Good job! Anything you do while thinking of God, loving Him, and doing it for Him with a good attitude is worship! You can worship Him in everything you do by the way you act and by being thankful! Can you think of any other ways you could worship God today?

Check it with the Word!

BIBLE

Psalm 95:6 tells us,

"Oh, come, let us worship and bow down; let us kneel before the LORD, our Maker!"

One of the reasons God made us was to worship Him.

KEY TRUTH:

I can worship God

I can worship God

<u>Copywork:</u> Let's copy our verse this week and think about some different ways we can worship God today!

Oh come, let us worship and bow down; let us kneel before the LORD, our Maker! (Psalm 95:6)

The Entry of Christ into Jerusalem by Pietro Lorenzetti (1320)

This picture is the story of Jesus coming into Jerusalem. You can see how people are gathering palm tree leaves and some are scattered under Jesus' feet. Someone is laying their cloak on the ground for Jesus to walk on. The disciples are behind Jesus and the crowd is in front. Many many people came to worship Jesus.

LET'S TAKE A CLOSER LOOK

Why do you think the boy is climbing the palm tree in the background? Why are they collecting palm branches? Can you count the disciples behind Jesus? How many do you count? What do you think it would have been like to watch Jesus come into your city? Where would you be if you could put yourself into this picture?

Art study

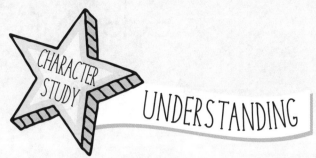

Understanding means taking the time to think about how someone else is feeling. To be an understanding person, you have to listen first to what someone else has to say and be able to understand their position and their opinion and their emotions. It's kind of like putting yourself in their shoes, imagining what it would feel like if you were them. First Corinthians 13:5 tells us that love does not insist on its own way.

♡ ♡ ♡ ♡ ♡ ♡ ♡ ♡ ♡ ♡ ♡ ♡ ♡ ♡ ♡

Let's learn more about what understanding means by looking at some similar words (synonyms) and opposite words (antonyms). Write your favorite two in the chart below.

Synonym		Antonym	
forgiving)		mean)	
patient)		selfish)	
kind)		unfeeling)	

Flash Card FUN
Make a flashcard with this week's character trait on it and decorate it however you want!

173

Name: _____

Day: 1 2 ③ 4

color it!

I am
UNDERSTANDING

WEEK 21: WHAT IS
WORSHIP?

174

draw it!

Remember when we talked about all the things that worship can be? Draw a picture of one of those things (look back if you need to). It could be you singing a song, or a musical instrument, or it could be helping someone or doing your chores.

Name: _____

Day: 1 2 3 ④

Can you remember our key truth for the week?

_____
- -
_____
_____
- -
_____

Write or narrate to your teacher one way you can worship God.

_____
- -
_____
_____
- -
_____
_____
- -
_____

NOT ON MY OWN STRENGTH...

Father, help me to be more understanding to others, to listen to their thoughts and consider how they are feeling.

journal entry Aliyah

Week Twenty-two: Works vs. Faith
Day: ① 2 3 4

Today I had a problem. I climbed the biggest tree I have ever climbed! I just kept on going up and up! Then my brother called me, and I looked down and all of a sudden I wasn't as excited anymore ... I was scared! The branches looked farther apart than I had remembered. I know I had gotten UP the tree, so I should be able to get down, but I was too scared! Dad came out to help, but he didn't climb the tree to get me like I thought he would. He stood at the bottom and said he would help me, but I had to come down one branch so he could reach me.

I laughed nervously as I reached my foot down toward the branch beneath me, but my toes didn't touch anything! I pulled my legs up and yelled for my dad. Dad said to try again, I was almost there. I had to trust that my dad would tell me the truth and that if he said the branch was there, it was. Finally, I dropped a little lower and my foot landed on the branch and, sure enough, my daddy grabbed me! I am glad my dad helped me and that I trusted him enough to listen, or I would have been stuck up there for a long time!

Aliyah

Name: _____

Day: ① 2 3 4

Why was Aliyah scared?

What did her dad tell her to do?

How do you think she felt after she listened to her dad and he grabbed her and carried her down to safety?

talk about it!

Part of being a Christian is believing God, or trusting Him, which we call faith. Ephesians 2:8 tells us that we are saved through faith, which is a gift from God. It is easy to say we believe something, but what shows if we do or not is when we act on that faith. Aliyah trusted her daddy because she knew him really well. She knew that he wouldn't lie to her and that he would help her. She showed that she believed her daddy by trusting him and putting her foot down on the branch. Faith in God is the same. We can say we believe God, but when we show that we believe God by our actions, THAT is faith!

Check it with the Word!

BIBLE

So also faith by itself, if it does not have works, is dead. (James 2:17)

James 1:22 tells us not just to listen to the Word of God, but to do what it says. We sometimes think that faith means to believe God, but it really means to trust Him, and if we don't show that we trust Him by the way we live our lives, then we don't really, truly trust Him.

KEY TRUTH:

Faith without works is dead

Faith without works is dead

Name: _____

Day: 1 ②3 4

Copywork: Copy the verse and think about how faith is shown through what we do.

So also faith by itself, if it does not have works, is dead. (James 2:17)

WEEK 22: WORKS
VS. FAITH

HYMN STUDY

Read the song, and circle or highlight the rhyming words.

MY FAITH LOOKS UP TO THEE

Hymn: verse one ➡️ Interpretation:

Hymn: verse one		Interpretation:
My faith looks up to Thee,	～	My hope and trust is in You, God
Thou Lamb of Calvary,	～	You, the Lamb who died on the Cross
Saviour Divine;	～	Perfect Saviour
Now hear me while I pray;	～	Hear my prayer
Take all my guilt away;	～	Take away my sin
Oh, let me from this day	～	And from today on
Be wholly Thine.	～	Make me Your child

talk about it!

This song is a prayer to God, asking Him to cleanse us from our sins, change us, remove fear from us, and inspire us. It is a beautiful song filled with lots of messages! What words mean the most to you and why?

You can explore this entire hymn with a line-by-line modern interpretation on pages 307-308.

WEEK 22: WORKS VS. FAITH

CHARACTER STUDY

HARD WORKING

To be hard working means that you do all you must to get things done. You don't just do the easiest job — you do the job the very best you can. God has lots to say about us being hard workers. Colossians 3:23 tells us to do everything with all our hearts, as if we were doing the job for God, not a person. Imagine cleaning your room not for your mom, but for God! And when we do something for God, working hard and having a good attitude, it is another way to worship Him, remember?

Let's learn more about what **hard working** means by looking at some similar words (synonyms) and opposite words (antonyms).

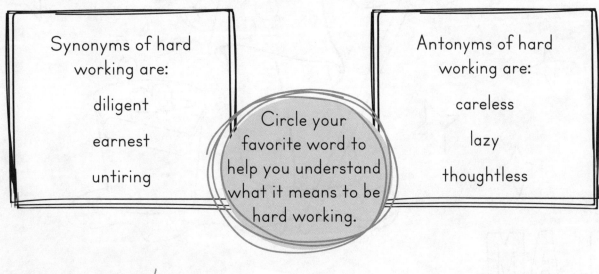

Synonyms of hard working are:

diligent

earnest

untiring

Circle your favorite word to help you understand what it means to be hard working.

Antonyms of hard working are:

careless

lazy

thoughtless

Flash Card FUN

Make a flashcard with this week's character trait on it and decorate it however you want!

WEEK 22: WORKS VS. FAITH

I AM

HARDWORKING

draw it!

Can you draw a picture of you working hard — cleaning your room or doing dishes or doing your schoolwork? What is one way you can practice having good work ethic this week?

Name: _____

Day: 1 2 3 ④

Can you remember our key truth for the week?

_____
- -
_____
- -
_____
- -
_____

Faith is the proof of what we hope for; it is the action showing what we believe in. Write the highlighted sentence on the lines below, then talk to your teacher about how faith is important in your life.

_____
- -
_____
- -
_____
- -
_____
- -
_____
- -
_____

NOT ON MY OWN STRENGTH...

God, thank You that You made me to be a hard worker. Bless the work of my hands that I might honor You with every job that I do. Help me to do it my very best, with a good attitude.

WEEK 22: WORKS VS. FAITH

journal entry **Malakai**

Daddy had to go away on a trip for some training. He will be gone for two whole weeks! That is a long time! He left today, and I was crying and hugging him, and then he told me that he had a present for me to help me feel better while he was gone. Presents sometimes make me a little bit less sad, and I was curious what it would be. I wiped my eyes and asked him, "What is it?" He told me that Mom would give it to me after he had left, and then he hugged all the other kids and my mom and drove away. I still felt sad, but kind of excited to see what present mom had for us in the house!

When we did our Bible reading in the morning, Mom read to us about when Jesus left His friends, the disciples, to go back to heaven. They were pretty sad too, and Jesus said the same thing as my daddy! That He would send them power when He sent the Holy Spirit, just like a present! Maybe that made them feel better too!

Malakai

talk about it!

Do presents make you feel better?

Do you remember who the Holy Spirit is?

Check it with the Word!

BIBLE

When we become a Christian, when we have a relationship with God and ask Him to be the Lord of our lives, we have the Holy Spirit with us, too! And the Holy Spirit has gifts, did you know that? I love gifts, don't you? Let's get out our Bibles. We are going to have our parent or teacher tell us what those gifts are.

To each is given the manifestation of the Spirit for the common good. For to one is given through the Spirit the utterance of wisdom, and to another the utterance of knowledge according to the same Spirit, to another faith by the same Spirit, to another gifts of healing by the one Spirit, to another the working of miracles, to another prophecy, to another the ability to distinguish between spirits, to another various kinds of tongues, to another the interpretation of tongues. All these are empowered by one and the same Spirit, who apportions to each one individually as he wills. (1 Corinthians 12:7–11)

There are nine different gifts in that passage! See if you can find them in the passage above and underline or circle them!

KEY TRUTH:

God gives gifts

God gives gifts
_____
_____
_____
_____
_____

Copywork: Let's copy part of 1 Corinthians 12:11.

... the ... Spirit ... distributes all
these gifts. (1 Corinthians 12:11 NLT)

Circle or highlight the rhyming words.

My Father Gives Good Gifts

My Father gives good gifts
To each and every one.
He uses me to help
His kingdom work get done.

The Holy Spirit helps
To give me what I need
To do the work He has for me,
To guide me and to lead.

My Father gives good gifts.
He is faithful all my days
To do what is the best
I can trust the Word He says.

talk
about it!

Can you find the rhythm? Read it one more time and this time clap out the rhythm of the poem.

Underline your favorite line.

Can you remember one of the gifts God gives?

WEEK 23: GIFTS OF THE SPIRIT

ENCOURAGER

Name: _____

Day: 1 2 ③ 4

Did you know that the Bible tells us to encourage one another? First Thessalonians 5:11 tells us, "Therefore encourage one another and build one another up." That means to speak kind and helpful and comforting words to each other. Words are a powerful thing — some words can make us feel really terrible, like if someone tells you that they don't want to play with you or you are weird. Other words can make us feel really happy and good, like when someone tells you that you are helpful or really good at something. Part of who God made us to be is encouraging and kind to one another.

Write these synonyms and antonyms for encourager in the correct column of the chart below.

support, upset, trouble, cheer, comfort, hurt

Synonyms:	Antonyms:

Flash Card FUN

Make a flashcard with this week's character trait on it and decorate it however you want!

189

I AM AN ENCOURAGER

Name: _____

Day: 1 2 3 ④

draw it!

Draw a picture of a present to remind you that God gives us gifts, too!

WEEK 23: GIFTS
OF THE SPIRIT

journal!

Can you remember our key truth for the week?

_____
_____
_____
_____

Write or narrate to your teacher one thing you can do to be an encourager today.

_____
_____
_____
_____
_____
_____

NOT ON MY OWN STRENGTH...

God, help me to encourage everyone
I meet today with my words and my
actions. Help me to be someone that
brings Your light and love.

I love looking at pictures. They remind me about all sorts of fun memories that I sometimes forget about. Today I was looking through pictures of when we went to the apple orchard in the fall. I LOVE apples. I love picking them from the tree and I REALLY love eating them! I remember riding on the tractor (which was really fun) and learning how to pick the apples "eye to the sky," with the bottom up so we didn't hurt the tree. They told us that the fruit grew best on the trees that had lots of water, pruning, and attention. It was hard work to help a tree produce apples. They had to take care of each tree!

But the trees didn't have to do very much work. If they were in the right place, in the right soil, with the right care, they were made to produce apples! Maybe that's like what Mom was talking about when she was talking about the fruit of the Spirit? We are made to be like God, in His image, but we need His help and care to do that! I am so thankful that God takes such good care of us!

Aliyah

Name: _____

Day: ① 2 3 4

talk
about it!

What do you think would happen if the apple trees didn't get water or sunlight? Do you think they would still have big, juicy apples? Why not?

Just like plants need sun and water and oxygen to grow and do what they are supposed to do, we need the Word of God and God's love and presence to grow and do what we are supposed to do!

Check it with the Word!

We have been learning about some different character traits each week, like how to be an encourager, or kind, or have self-control. Some of those traits are actually called the fruit of the Spirit, which means they are the result of spending time with God. As we spend time reading the Bible and praying and being with God, we will be changed to be more like Him. There are nine different fruits of the Spirit. Open up your Bible to Galatians 5:22—23 with me:

> But the fruit of the Spirit is love, joy, peace, patience, kindness, goodness, faithfulness, gentleness, self-control. . . .

Can you underline or highlight each fruit of being close to God?

KEY TRUTH:

The Holy Spirit helps me

The Holy Spirit helps me

_____

_____

_____

_____

Copywork: Today, we are going to copy all the fruit of the Spirit to help us learn them. Ready?

Love

Joy

Peace

Patience

Kindness

Goodness

Gentleness

Faithfulness

Self-control

Apple picking at Eragny-sur-Epte by Camille Pissarro (1888)

This is a painting set in the 1800s that shows people picking apples. Notice the women are picking up the apples that have fallen on the ground. What do you think the man is doing with the long stick?

LET'S TAKE A CLOSER LOOK

Lighting, shadows, and color can often help to create a mood or feeling when looking at a painting. They also help to create the setting (where the painting is or when). What time of year do you think this is? What time of day?

This painting by Pissarro uses what was, at the time, a fairly new painting technique called pointillism. If you look closely you can see that instead of blending the colors together and painting in long, smooth strokes, it uses very short dabs or strokes of different colors that blend together to create color and contrast and form a less detailed picture on the canvas. When you see fruit from now on try and remember the fruit of the Spirit.

Art study

CHARACTER STUDY

LOVING

To be a loving person means that you are thinking about someone, you want good things for them, and you take care of them. Sometimes we think love is an emotion, something we feel, but we know that God IS love and love comes from Him. So it is not really something we feel as much as something we show and choose to do. God commands us to love one another in John 13:34. We can't be commanded to feel something, can we? But we can choose to think about someone and take care of them, even if we don't feel like it. That is what it means to be loving — to think of other people more than yourself, and we learned yesterday that love is a fruit of the Spirit. That means that the more time we spend with Jesus, the more God's love will pour out of us and the easier it will be to love people . . . even when it's hard!

Let's learn more about what loving means by looking at some similar words (synonyms) and opposite words (antonyms). Circle your favorite two.

Synonyms	Antonyms
friendly	hateful
warm	mean
caring	selfish

Flash Card FUN
Make a flashcard with this week's character trait on it and decorate it however you want!

197

WEEK 24: FRUIT OF THE SPIRIT

I AM
LOVING

Name: _____

Day: 1 2 3 ④

draw it!

Draw a picture of a tree with fruit on it — any kind of fruit. If you want, you can write the fruit of the Spirit on the fruit to help you remember them!

journal!

Can you remember our key truth for the week?

_____
_____
_____
_____

Write some ways that you can show love to someone in your family.

_____
_____
_____
_____
_____
_____

NOT ON MY OWN STRENGTH . . .

Thank You, Lord, that You are the author of love. Thank You that You can help me love my family, my friends, and even people I don't get along with very well! Help me to be more loving this week!

WEEK 24: FRUIT OF THE SPIRIT

My daddy is a police officer and he knows all about rules. Part of his job is to help make sure that people keep rules. Rules that keep us safe — like not driving too fast or wearing our seatbelts. He told me that everything we do has a consequence. Like when I disobeyed and was jumping on the couch, I fell down and hurt myself. He told me that the rule to not jump on the couch was to keep me safe, and the consequence was that I hurt myself.

The Old Testament has lots of laws and rules, and today we learned about the Ten Commandments. Those are kind of like 10 rules that God gave to Moses to help people remember how they should live. Even though sometimes rules can be hard or frustrating, my dad said they are usually there for a good reason. My dad is usually right. . . .

Malakai

Name: _____

Day: ① 2 3 4

talk about it!

Do you think rules are a good thing?

Are there some rules you don't like?

Can you think of a consequence that happened when you didn't follow the rules?

Check it with the Word!

Open your Bible and read Exodus 20:3-17.
This version is from the *International Children's Bible:*

"You must not have any other gods except me.

You must not make for yourselves any idols . . . You must not worship or serve any idol . . . .

You must not use the name of the Lord your God thoughtlessly. The Lord will punish anyone who is guilty and misuses his name.

Remember to keep the Sabbath as a holy day . . . .

Honor your father and your mother . . . .

You must not murder anyone.

You must not be guilty of adultery.

You must not steal.

You must not tell lies . . . .

. . . You must not want to take anything that belongs to your neighbor."

KEY TRUTH:

I follow God's commands

I follow God's commands

_____
_____
_____
_____
_____

Copywork: Copy the first of the Ten Commandments below.

You must not have any other gods
except me. (Exodus 20:3 ICB)

WEEK 25: THE TEN COMMANDMENTS

Name: _____

Day: 1 ② 3 4

Listen to your parent or teacher read the songs and circle or highlight the rhyming words together.

VICTORY IN JESUS

Hymn: verse one		Interpretation:
I heard an old, old story,		I heard an old story
How a Savior came from glory,		How someone came to save us
How He gave His life on Calvary		How He died on the Cross
To save a wretch like me;		To save a sinner like me
I heard about His groaning,		I heard about His sadness
Of His precious blood's atoning		And how His blood saved us
Then I repented of my sins;		Then I said sorry for my sins
And won the victory.		And I won eternal life!

This song is about what Jesus did for us — that even though we make mistakes, Jesus gave His life and we have victory (or we win over the consequence of our sins). What amazes you the most about all Jesus has done for us?

talk about it!

You can explore this entire hymn with a line-by-line modern interpretation on pages 311-312.

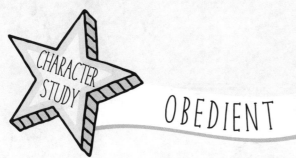

CHARACTER STUDY

OBEDIENT

One of the Ten Commandments is to honor your mother and father. One way to honor them is to obey them. Being obedient means that you do what your parents tell you. When you get older, you will still sometimes need to obey your boss, the law, or the rules. Learning how to obey even when we don't feel like it isn't easy, but did you know that when you obey your parents, God has a promise for you? Exodus 20:12 says to honor your parents so that your life may be long.

Let's learn more about what it means to obey by looking at some similar words (synonyms) and opposite words (antonyms). Write these words in the correct column of the chart below.

argue, accept, agree, disagree, oppose, follow

Synonyms:	Antonyms:

Flash Card FUN
Make a flashcard with this week's character trait on it and decorate it however you want!

205

Name:

Day: 1 2 ③ 4

color it!

I AM OBEDIENT

WEEK 25: THE TEN
COMMANDMENTS

Name:

Day: 1 2 ③ 4

color it!

I AM OBEDIENT

WEEK 25: THE TEN COMMANDMENTS

Name: _____

Day: 1 2 3 ④

draw it!

Draw a picture of a time you obeyed your mom or dad. Maybe they asked you to clean your room and you did, or they told you not to ride your bike without your helmet and you remembered to wear it!

journal!

Can you remember our key truth for the week?

_____
_____
_____
_____

Write a sentence or two about your picture.

_____
_____
_____
_____
_____
_____

NOT ON MY OWN STRENGTH...

Jesus, help me to obey when I am told to do something — to honor my parents by respecting them and listening to what they say. Thank You that You can help me remember when I forget.

It was my birthday yesterday, and I got a brand new bike from Mommy and Daddy! It is blue and white and has a little bell on the front, and I can't stop riding it! I have been riding up and down the street and even on the grass and some hills. I love my new bike!

I was riding down a little hill on our grass when I saw a hole in the ground. I quickly swerved so that I wouldn't hit the hole, but then my bike got really wobbly and it fell down. It didn't really hurt on the grass, but my head landed on a rock and it cracked my helmet. I wasn't hurt, but Mom said we need to buy a new helmet! It is really important to wear a helmet — it protected my head from getting hurt!

Aliyah

talk about it!

Why do you think Aliyah's helmet was important?

Can you think of any other things that help protect you that you might wear?

Check it with the Word!

Do you know that God says we have spiritual armor, too? Just like we have helmets and knee pads and work gloves and different things that help protect our bodies, God says that we have armor that we can wear to protect our hearts, minds, and spirits!

Open up your Bible to Ephesians 6:11–17 and let's see if we can underline the armor:

Put on the whole armor of God, that you may be able to stand against the schemes of the devil. For we do not wrestle against flesh and blood, but against the rulers, against the authorities, against the cosmic powers over this present darkness, against the spiritual forces of evil in the heavenly places. Therefore take up the whole armor of God, that you may be able to withstand in the evil day, and having done all, to stand firm. Stand therefore, having fastened on the belt of truth, and having put on the breastplate of righteousness, and, as shoes for your feet, having put on the readiness given by the gospel of peace. In all circumstances take up the shield of faith, with which you can extinguish all the flaming darts of the evil one; and take the helmet of salvation, and the sword of the Spirit, which is the word of God. . .

KEY TRUTH:

Put on the armor of God

Put on the armor of God
_____
_____
_____
_____
_____

Copywork: Choose ONE PART of the armor of God and copy it onto the lines below.

Belt of truth

Breastplate of righteousness

Shoes for your feet to bring peace

Shield of faith

Helmet of salvation

Sword of the Spirit

Name: _____

Day: 1 (2) 3 4

Read this poem about
the Armor of God

Poetry

The Armor of God

Put on the full armor of God
So that you may stand your ground.
The belt of truth certain and strong
Around your waist be wound.

The breastplate of righteousness
   over your heart
Gleaming and clean and bright,
For you have been washed in the
   blood of Christ
So that God may declare you right.

The gospel of peace on your feet
Ready to move and to do
The example of Jesus leading you on
To live the life He showed you to.

The shield of faith firm in your grasp
Your action that proves you believe,
To protect you from the evil one
And the struggles you will receive.

The helmet of salvation firm on your
   head
A free gift that cannot be taken,
To protect your mind from the lie
That God's redemption can ever be
   shaken.

The sword of the Spirit held fast in
   your hands
The Word of God is steadfast and
   true.
Keep it fresh in your mind and
   pressed on your heart
A soldier, trained for what God
   has for you.

talk
about it!

Circle or highlight the rhyming words.

Can you find the rhythm? Read it one more time and this time
clap out the rhythm of the poem.

Underline your favorite line.

Can you remember a part of the armor of God?

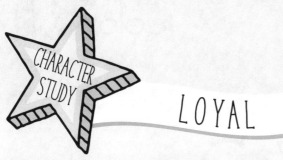

CHARACTER STUDY

LOYAL

Loyal means that you are on someone's side. That you stick with someone. Proverbs 18:24 tells us that there is a friend who sticks closer than a brother. A true friend, a loyal friend, who will always be there, who is dependable (remember, that word?). You can be loyal to your family, loyal to your friends, loyal to your job, etc.

Let's learn more about what it means to be **loyal** by looking at some similar words (synonyms) and opposite words (antonyms). Circle your favorite 2 synonyms and antonyms.

trustworthy   unreliable

true   **LOYAL**   disloyal

behind someone   unfaithful

Flash Card FUN
Make a flashcard with this week's character trait on it and decorate it however you want!

213

Name:

Day: 1 2 ③ 4

color it!

I AM LOYAL

WEEK 26: ARMOR OF GOD

214

draw it!

Draw a picture of the armor of God (or your favorite part of the armor — maybe the sword or the helmet).

journal!

Can you remember our key truth for the week?

_____
_____
_____
_____

Write about which piece of armor you drew.

_____
_____
_____
_____
_____
_____
_____

NOT ON MY OWN STRENGTH...

God, help me to become more loyal, to be someone that people can count on. Thank You that You are changing me to be more like You.

WEEK 26: ARMOR OF GOD

We have learned SO much about what it means to be a Christian, but we don't want to forget it! Each week, you have learned a key truth! Today, we are going to play a game to help us remember what they are.

Pull out pages 327-329 for Quarter 3 and cut out your Key Truth cards. There are lots of ways to help you remember your key truths. You can hop on each card and try to remember what it is or say what it means to you. You can ask a parent to read the first part and see if you can remember the end. You can copy them out and you can decorate them! Think of a fun way you can review your key truths!

If you have been working on your character trait flashcards, this is the week you get to practice them all together! There are so many fun ways to do this! You can practice them on your own by just reading them through or you can play a game to make it more fun! You can even play a game with a family member or friend. You can take turns reading the character trait and have the other person say an example, act it out, or explain what it means. Then trade places! You can make another copy of your cards (or have a parent help) and play memory by turning them all over and trying to find matching pairs. You can even put them on the floor in a pattern or build an obstacle course and as you find the cards or land on the cards, say what it is or what it means OR an example of that character trait.

SO many fun ways to review your cards! Choose one or make up your own and see how well you can remember what these character traits look like in action!

Name: _____

Day: 1 ②3 4

Highlight, circle, or color the words in the puzzle below.

E	B	W	P	K	L	E	W	Y	H	H	D	X	X
P	J	I	M	L	Q	G	M	C	S	C	W	D	Q
I	X	W	O	R	K	I	N	G	W	B	W	Q	Y
A	B	E	O	Z	W	U	Q	J	J	T	T	S	F
H	F	J	D	Y	O	B	E	D	I	E	N	T	O
O	Q	E	N	C	O	U	R	A	G	E	R	G	P
F	L	O	V	I	N	G	P	R	Z	M	A	X	N
F	Y	W	B	H	A	R	D	M	N	S	O	Y	R
U	U	N	D	E	R	S	T	A	N	D	I	N	G
R	S	J	N	A	D	A	P	T	A	B	L	E	D
T	R	U	S	T	W	O	R	T	H	Y	U	J	Z
L	O	Y	A	L	E	E	V	A	Z	Z	C	R	D

ADAPTABLE   LOYAL   UNDERSTANDING
ENCOURAGER   OBEDIENT   HARD WORKING
LOVING   TRUSTWORTHY

To help us reflect on what we have learned about this quarter, we are going to do a creative connection, or artistic, hands-on project! This is optional. If you prefer, you can draw a picture or use playdough or something else to show what you learned.

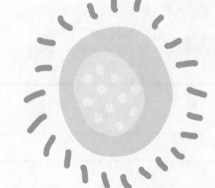

Name: _____

Day: 1 2 ③ 4

LET'S CONNECT creatively

WHOLE FAMILY ACTIVITY

Armor of God

Supplies needed:

- paint (any kind you have around)

- construction paper or cardboard (cereal boxes work great)

- paintbrushes, marker or pen

- scissors

- glue gun

Instructions: Today we are going to make a our very own armor! This is going to help us remember what each piece of armor represents. You can use paper or cardboard or whatever you have around your house. Here is a list of the armor!

Belt of truth

Breastplate of righteousness

Shoes of the gospel of peace

Shield of faith

Helmet of salvation

Sword of the Spirit

1. Have a parent or teacher use a pencil to sketch out some simple armor pieces.

2. Staple or glue your pieces together. You can be as detailed or as simple as you'd like!

3. Write or paint the names of each piece of armor to help you remember what they mean.

WEEK 27: REVIEW

journal!

What is your strongest character trait?

_____

_____

_____

Which one do you need to work on the most?

_____

_____

_____

What is your favorite thing you learned about being a Christian?

_____

_____

_____

QUARTER 4
The Great Relationship

I was at the park today, and I met a new friend named John. We were playing a really fun game where we had to stay off the ground! Running, jumping, sliding, hanging — all my favorite things! It was sunny and warm and we were having so much fun. Then John and I bumped into each other and he fell off the slide and hurt himself. He wasn't hurt too bad, but he got mad at me. I said I was sorry, but he wouldn't talk to me. The rest of the time I was at the park, I tried talking to him and he kept walking away from me or pretending I wasn't there. I got really sad and went to talk to my mom about it. She said that it was just because he was frustrated and maybe he needed to have some time to himself for a while, so I played with my brother instead. Just before we left, John came over and said he was sorry for not talking to me. I felt terrible that he got hurt, but even more terrible when I felt like he didn't want to listen to me.

Malakai

talk about it!

Have you ever felt like someone wasn't listening to you?

How did it make you feel?

Day: ① 2 3 4

Do you know that God loves to have conversations with us? Not only does He want to listen to us and hear us pray to Him, but He also wants to talk back to us.

Let's open our Bibles to John 10:27.

My sheep hear my voice, and I know them, and they follow me.

Now let's look at John 8:47.

Whoever is of God hears the words of God.

These verses show us that God speaks to us. Did you know that God spoke in many different ways in the Bible?

God spoke through people like when God used prophets in the Bible. (Hebrews 1:1)

God spoke through the Bible. (Hebrews 4:12)

God spoke in dreams like with Joseph in the Bible. (Genesis 37:5)

God spoke in visions like He did with John. (Revelation 1:1-2)

The important thing to know about hearing God's voice is that He will never contradict the Bible, so the Bible is like our tester. It is how we know if it is really God speaking or not. If what we are feeling or thinking or hearing goes against Scripture, it isn't God.

KEY TRUTH:

God speaks to me

God speaks to me
_____
_____
_____
_____

Name: _____

Day: 1 ② 3 4

Copywork: Let's copy part of John 10:27.

My sheep hear my voice . . .
(John 10:27)

Moses and the Burning Bush by Raphael Sanzio (1483–1520)

This painting shows God speaking to Moses from the burning bush. Notice how the artist keeps the main focus on Moses, with his face down, rather than on God. It would be pretty hard to draw God, wouldn't it?

LET'S TAKE A CLOSER LOOK

Let's see how many colors we can find in this painting! Notice how even little changes in how dark or light a color is can make the picture more interesting.

Point to some of the shadows and some of the light spots.

How does Moses look like he is feeling?

How does this painting make you feel?

Art study

CHARACTER STUDY

GIVING

To be giving is kind of like the opposite of greedy. It means that you give freely to people; you aren't selfish. The Bible tells us in 2 Corinthians 9:7 that God loves a cheerful giver. God sees our hearts. He doesn't just look for what we do but why we are doing it — for attention, or out of love?

Let's learn more about what it means to be giving by looking up some similar words (synonyms) and opposite words (antonyms).

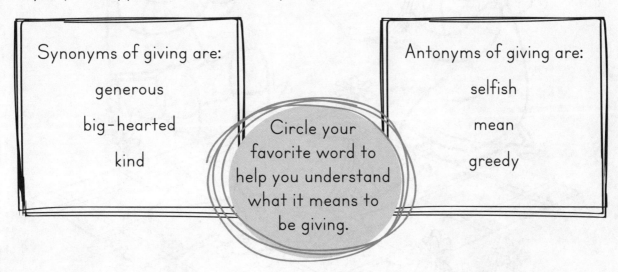

Synonyms of giving are:

generous

big-hearted

kind

Circle your favorite word to help you understand what it means to be giving.

Antonyms of giving are:

selfish

mean

greedy

Flash Card FUN

Make a flashcard with this week's character trait on it and decorate it however you want!

227

I AM GIVING

Name: _____

Day: 1 2 3 ④

draw it!

Draw a picture of the burning bush. Use the painting or your own imagination. What do you think it would be like? Read the story in Exodus 3 if you want more ideas.

journal!

Name: _____

Day: 1 2 3 ④

Can you remember our key truth for the week?

_____
. . . .
_____
_____
. . . .
_____

What is one way you can be giving today?

_____
. . . .
_____
. . . .
_____
_____
. . . .
_____

NOT ON MY OWN STRENGTH...

Jesus, You are the most giving person there ever was. You gave Your life to save us. Thank You for what You did for me. Help me to become more like You — to be more giving and love people the way You love them.

My favorite game is hide and seek. I love it when my mommy and daddy play with us. We run all over the house hiding in the silliest places we can think of. I sometimes help Janiah because she is only four. I don't know what is more fun . . . finding someone I have been looking all over for or being the person who is found. Sometimes when my daddy finds me, he tickles me and then carries me around the house looking for the other people who are hiding. I wish we could play it every night!

Aliyah

Name: _____

Day: ① 2 3 4

talk about it!

Do you like playing hide and seek?

What is your favorite part about it? Hiding, being found, or both?

Check it with the Word!

BIBLE

Do you know that God talks a little bit about hide and seek? He tells us to seek multiple times in the Bible, and He talks about searching for us like the shepherd looks for his lost lamb. Let's open up our Bibles and find an example.

Ask, and it will be given to you; seek, and you will find; knock, and it will be opened to you. For everyone who asks receives, and the one who seeks finds, and to the one who knocks it will be opened. (Matthew 7:7–8)

God could just tell you everything about Himself, couldn't He? He could make you love Him if He wanted to, but He wants you to choose. He doesn't force us to love Him. He gives us the choice of whom we will follow. He doesn't force us to have a relationship with Him, He lets us choose how close we want to get to Him. He plays a little game of hide and seek sometimes, kind of like He is saying, "Come and get me! I'm right here and I have a little bit more to show you!" If you want to be closer to God and understand His words even better, all you have to do is ask Him!

KEY TRUTH:

Seek and you will find

Seek and you will find

_____
_____
_____
_____
_____

Copywork: Have your parent or teacher underline a section or all of the reference below for you to copy.

Seek, and you will find; knock, and it will be opened to you. (Matthew 7:7)

WEEK 29: HIDE AND SEEK

Name: _____

Day: 1 ②③ 4

Read the verse, and circle or highlight the rhyming words.

SEEK YE FIRST

Hymn: verse three ➡ Interpretation:

Ask and it shall be given unto you	∼	Ask and you will have it
Seek and ye shall find	∼	Look and you will find it
Knock and the door shall be opened unto you	∼	Knock on the door and it will open
Allelu Alleluia	∼	Praise God!

talk about it!

This song is Scripture put to words. It is all about seeking God, just like we were talking about yesterday!

Why is it so good for us when we seek God?

You can explore this entire hymn with a line-by-line modern interpretation on page 313.

WEEK 29: HIDE AND SEEK

CHARACTER STUDY

HELPFUL

When you are helpful, it also means that you are being considerate of other people — that you are thinking about their needs and helping even when you don't feel like it. It isn't always easy, but every time you practice helping someone with a good attitude, it helps you grow to be a more helpful person!

Let's learn more about what it means to be **helpful** by looking up some similar words (synonyms) and opposite words (antonyms). Circle your favorite two and write them on the chart below.

Synonyms:	Antonyms:
supportive, caring, useful	unwilling, selfish, lazy

Flash Card FUN
Make a flashcard with this week's character trait on it and decorate it however you want!

235

Name:

Day: 1 2 ③ 4

color it!

I AM HELPFUL

WEEK 29: HIDE AND SEEK

Name: _____

Day: 1 2 3 ④

Let's think of something that will remind us to seek God. Maybe binoculars or a picture of you playing hide and seek!

WEEK 29: HIDE AND SEEK

journal!

Can you remember our key truth for the week?

What is one way you can seek God?

NOT ON MY OWN STRENGTH...

Thank You that You love me and
want me to be more like You.
Help me to show who You are by
noticing other people's needs and
helping them when they need me.

I went outside today all by myself. Now that spring is here, it is warmer outside, and I went to go sit on the hill in our backyard. I love going to the hill. That is where I sit down in the grass, and sometimes I just think, sometimes I talk to God, sometimes I just look at the clouds, and other times I go there to cry when I am sad. Today while I was sitting in the grass, I remembered a Bible verse from Sunday school, "Draw near to God, and He will draw near to you," James 4:8. Sometimes I think that God is far away, in heaven. Some days I even feel lonely and am not sure God can even hear me. But the Bible tells me that God will never leave me (Deuteronomy 31:6).

Even when I am alone, God is with me. If I call out to Him, He is there. He is not far away, He is with me always! Sometimes it's hard to remember that God is there all the time when I can't see Him. But the more I read my Bible and pray, the more I keep thinking about Him.

Malakai

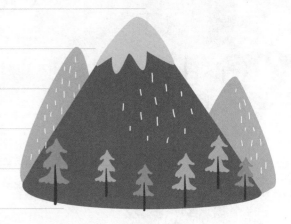

talk about it!

Do you ever talk to God all by yourself?

Have you ever felt that God is far away?

Check it with the Word!

BIBLE

God isn't far away. In fact, He can be everywhere all at once. That is why we know we can believe Him when He says He will be with us always. ALWAYS. He will never leave us nor forsake us. Open up your Bible to Matthew 28:20.

And behold, I am with you always, to the end of the age.

God wants to have a relationship with you. He wants to be a part of your life when you are doing your chores or doing your school work or reading a new book. He wants to be included in everything you do, because He is always with you!

KEY TRUTH:

God wants me close

God wants me close

Name: _____

Day: 1 ②3 4

Copywork: Write out the words of Matthew 28:20 below.

I am with you always, to the end of the age. (Matthew 28:20)

Poetry

Read this poem.

I am waiting

In the quiet places of your heart
Where no one knows to seek,
I watch you live your days in
    motion —
I watch, I wait, I speak.

When you are with your friends
Or getting out of bed,
Do you know that I am there?
I am the one who lifts your head.

Did you hear I'll never leave you?
I am with you every day,
When you're talking or you're
    playing,
By your side I'll stay.

I am with you in the silly.
I am with you in the fun.
I am with you in the hard times.
I won't leave what I've begun.

You are my precious child,
I love to be with you,
To meet you in your daily life.
When you go out, I will come too.

talk about it!

Circle the rhyming words

Who do you think is talking in the poem? That is called the point of view.

Do you think that God is with you all the time?

Sometimes it's easy to forget that He is with us! He wants to be with you even when you are playing games or doing school! He doesn't just want to meet you when you are praying for a meal or before you go to bed! He wants to be a part of every part of your day!

WEEK 30: DRAW NEAR TO ME

242

CHARACTER STUDY

INTEGRITY

Integrity means to do what is right even when no one is watching. To be a person of integrity means that you do the right thing with the right motivation. You aren't just obeying your mom because you want a prize, or you want someone to say "good job." You would obey your mom even if no one knew you were doing it and no one cared ... because it is the right thing to do! God doesn't sin. He always does what is right, and Jesus showed us what it means to live with integrity — to be someone who does what is right no matter what the consequence, no matter what the reward.

Let's learn more about what it means to have **integrity** by looking at some similar words (synonyms) and opposite words (antonyms). Copy two of your favorite in the correct column.

Synonym		Antonym	
honest)		dishonest)	
purity)		disgrace)	
goodness)		false)	

Flash Card FUN
Make a flashcard with this week's character trait on it and decorate it however you want!

WEEK 30: DRAW NEAR TO ME

Name: _____

Day: 1 2 ③ 4

color it!

I HAVE INTEGRITY

WEEK 30: DRAW
NEAR TO ME

draw it!

Can you draw a picture of something you do every day? Maybe it is brushing your teeth or doing your school work or eating food. Write on your drawing "I am with you always" to help you remember that God is with you even when you are doing normal things.

journal!

Can you remember our key truth for the week?

_____
- - - - - - - - - - - - - - - - -
_____
_____
- - - - - - - - - - - - - - - - -
_____

Choose one line of the poem (or more) and write it on the lines below.

_____
- - - - - - - - - - - - - - - - -
_____
_____
- - - - - - - - - - - - - - - - -
_____
_____

NOT ON MY OWN STRENGTH . . .

I want to be someone who lives with integrity, who does what is right for the right reasons. Help me to have a right heart in everything I do.

WEEK 30: DRAW
NEAR TO ME

My chore today was to fold a load of laundry and put it away. Our family has lots and lots of laundry because there are lots of people! I don't really like folding laundry, so I decided to make a game and talk to God while I was doing it! I talked to Him about my day and that I didn't really feel like doing laundry, but the more I talked to Him the more I just felt happy in my heart. Even though I was tired and didn't really want to do the chore, I started to have fun! I started singing one of my favorite worship songs, "In the River," and dancing while I put clothes away, and the more I sang, the more joy I felt! My whole day was better, and I knew that God was with me even while I helped my mom.

Aliyah

Name: _____

Day: ① 2 3 4

How did Aliyah feel before she started doing the chore?

Did she like doing laundry?

Do you ever not want to do your chores?

What helped Aliyah do her chore with a good attitude?

• •

Check it with the Word!

The Bible tells us that we can talk to God all the time, and that we should talk to God all the time. We learned last week that God is with us always and that He wants to be a part of everything we do. One of the ways we can include Him in our day is to talk to Him. We can talk to Him while we are doing our chores, when we are angry or sad or hurt — anytime!

Rejoice always, pray without ceasing, give thanks in all circumstances; for this is the will of God in Christ Jesus for you. (1 Thessalonians 5:16–18)

Ceasing means stopping, so "pray without ceasing" means to pray without stopping, to give thanks in all things, even when we are doing something we don't want to! We can have a thankful heart and pray to God, and He can help us to have joy even in the hard stuff!

• •

KEY TRUTH:

Pray all the time

Pray all the time
_____
_____
_____
_____

Copywork: Write out the words to I Thessalonians 5:17 and think about spending time in prayer today.

Pray without ceasing.
(1 Thessalonians 5:17)

Suspense by Charles Burton Barber (1845–1894)

Art study

This is a painting of a little girl praying before she eats her meal. Beside her are her two pets who look like they are very interested in sharing the food with her! The artist, Charles Burton Barber, was famous for showing the relationship between children and their pets.

LET'S TAKE A CLOSER LOOK

Notice the details on the cup, the wallpaper, the lace on the nightgown, and the curtain around her bed.

Point to the shadows and lighter areas in the painting.

Can you give the cat and dog names?

Why do you think there are flowers on the bed? They look like they are a present, wrapped in paper. Who do you think they are from? Do you pray and give thanks for your meal?

WEEK 31: PRAY
ALL THE TIME

CONFIDENT

Name: _____

Day: 1 2 ③ 4

To be confident means that you know who you are and what you are capable of. If you are good at a sport or can play the piano, you might be confident that you can play the game or the instrument because you have practiced and you know what you can do. The Bible tells us that the only thing that we can depend on, the only thing that won't let us down, the only thing that we can trust is Christ and who we are in Him. Jeremiah 17:7 tells us to put our confidence, or trust, in the Lord. We can be confident in God's faithfulness, in His promises, and in who we are in Him: His child, adopted into His family.

Write these synonyms and antonyms for **confident** in the correct column of the chart below.

bold, fear, doubt, courage, timid, trust

Synonyms:	Antonyms:

Flash Card FUN

Make a flashcard with this week's character trait on it and decorate it however you want!

WEEK 31: PRAY ALL THE TIME

I AM CONFIDENT

What is something to help you think of praying or talking to God? Some ideas are hands, a speech bubble, or you talking.

journal!

Can you remember our key truth for the week?

We learned this week to pray without ceasing. To have an ongoing conversation with God because He is always with us! What are some things you could talk to God about right now?

NOT ON MY OWN STRENGTH . . .

God, thank You that I can depend on You, that I can trust You no matter what! Help me not to depend on myself, but to depend on You — to be confident in who YOU say I am, not who I say I am.

WEEK 31: PRAY
ALL THE TIME

Today I went for a ride on my dirt bike. My dad came too. He rode the quad, and my brother and I went behind on our dirt bikes. Mom sent us to go gather some interesting plants that we could use in our nature journaling. I had my backpack and magnifying glass and even a bag to put what I found in, and we were off! Zooming over hills and grass and around logs and into the forest we went! When we stopped, Caleb and I got off our bikes, took off our helmets, and went into the forest a little ways. "Dad, come here!" I yelled. I found a vine that was wrapped all the way around a tree. There were leaves and stems everywhere, and it was already green, which means it must have grown really fast!

My dad took out his pocket knife and cut off a piece for me to put in my bag to take home to Mom and my sisters. I can't wait to learn more about vines. I wonder how fast they grow!

Malakai

Name: _____

Day: ① 2 3 4

talk about it!

Do you know what a vine is? A really good example is a grape vine. It is kind of like a little tree, and shoots of leaves come off of it and wrap around something tall and strong, and when the season is right, the branches make grapes! Yummy!

Check it with the Word!

BIBLE

God talks a lot about plants in the Bible! He tells us in John 15:5 that Jesus is the vine and we are the branches, and that we will produce fruit if we are in relationship with Him.

In Colossians 2:6–7, He tells us to be rooted in Him (Jesus) and established in the faith. Roots get their food from the ground. So if we are rooted in Him, then we are getting fed in Him. How do you think we can get fed in Jesus? Through His Word!

Deuteronomy 8:3 tells us that we don't "live by bread alone, but . . . by every word that comes from the mouth of the LORD." The Word of God is our food. If we memorize, think about, and spend time reading the Word of God, then we will be rooted in Him just like a plant! We will produce fruit if we have relationship with Him and, just like a vine, we will be healthy and safely held by the branches that hold us up — Jesus!

Therefore, as you received Christ Jesus the Lord, so walk in him, rooted and built up in him and established in the faith, just as you were taught, abounding in thanksgiving. (Colossians 2:6–7)

KEY TRUTH:

My roots are in Jesus

My roots are in Jesus

_____
_____
_____
_____

Copywork: Copy the words below and think about how we need God.

Rooted and built up in Him.
(Colossians 2:7)

Name: _____

Day: 1 ② 3 4

Listen to your parent or teacher read the song and circle or highlight the rhyming words together.

THOU TRUE VINE, THAT HEALS THE NATIONS

Hymn: verse one   →   Interpretation:

Hymn: verse one	Interpretation:
Thou true Vine, that heals the nations,	You are the vine that heals us
Tree of life, thy branches we.	You are the tree of the life we are the branches
They who leave thee fade and wither,	Those who leave you, are like leaves that change and dry in the fall
none bear fruit except in thee.	We only produce fruit with you
Cleanse us, make us sane and simple,	Clean us, renew our minds
till we merge our lives in thine,	Until we live like you, with you
gain ourselves in thee, the Vintage,	We find ourselves in you, the source
give ourselves through thee, the Vine.	Use us, through you—the vine

talk about it!

This song is based on John 15 where Jesus says that He is the vine and we are the branches. Why is it important for a branch to stay connected to a tree?

You can explore this entire hymn with a line-by-line modern interpretation on page 315.

WEEK 32: ROOTED IN THE VINE

CHARACTER STUDY

FAIR

Have you ever shared something with someone and given yourself the bigger piece? To be fair would be to make sure they are equal, that no one is getting more or less than the other person. Another word for fair is to be just and to judge rightly. There are lots of verses about God being just. James 2:1 tells us to show no partiality, which means favoritism, or not to be nicer to someone because you like them more. We are to be fair, or just, in our actions, our decisions, and even with our love.

Let's learn more about what it means to be fair by looking at some synonyms and antonyms of the word. Circle your favorite 2 words.

honest   dishonest

proper   **FAIR**   unjust

just   not equal

Flash Card FUN
Make a flashcard with this week's character trait on it and decorate it however you want!

259

color it!

I AM FAIR

Name: _____

Day: 1 2 3 ④

draw it!

Can you draw a picture of a plant: a grapevine or a tree? This is to help you remember that we need to be rooted or attached to Jesus and have a relationship with Him! Or (optional) go on a nature walk to find a plant and draw it in the box!

WEEK 32: ROOTED
IN THE VINE

Name: _____

Day: 1 2 3 ④

Can you remember our key truth for the week?

_____
- - - - - - - - - - - - - - - - - - -
_____
_____
- - - - - - - - - - - - - - - - - - -
_____

Can you write or narrate to your parent/teacher a way that you can be fair?

_____
- - - - - - - - - - - - - - - - - - -
_____
_____
- - - - - - - - - - - - - - - - - - -
_____
_____
- - - - - - - - - - - - - - - - - - -
_____

NOT ON MY OWN STRENGTH ...

You are the one who is just and fair. You love everyone equally, God. Help me to learn to be more fair, to think about what is right, not just what I want.

WEEK 32: ROOTED IN THE VINE

At Sunday school this week, we learned a new Bible verse that Mrs. Drycke told us we should memorize. I have been reading it over and over, trying to learn it, and want to write it in my journal to help me remember. "Finally, brothers, whatever is true, whatever is honorable, whatever is just, whatever is pure, whatever is lovely, whatever is commendable, if there is any excellence, if there is anything worthy of praise, think about these things" (Philippians 4:8). I think that this means to spend my time thinking about good things. Sometimes I spend my time thinking about how mad I am, or feeling sorry for myself that I can't have something I want. I guess what I think about is important.

Aliyah

Name: _____

Day: ① 2 3 4

Do you sometimes spend your time thinking about things that make you kind of mad or feeling sorry for yourself?

Do you think it's easy to focus on good things or something that takes practice?

Check it with the Word!

One of the best things we can think about that is good and pure and lovely and excellent and all the things we read about in Aliyah's journal is the Bible. That is a pretty good thing to think about, isn't it?

Let's open our Bibles to Joshua:

This Book of the Law shall not depart from your mouth, but you shall meditate on it day and night, so that you may be careful to do according to all that is written in it. For then you will make your way prosperous, and then you will have good success. (Joshua 1:8)

Do you know what meditate means? It means to think about. And not just quickly think about, but to keep it in your mind; to consider what it means or what it could mean; to process it. The Book of Law is the Bible, and when we spend our time thinking about it, it changes us. It renews our minds and changes the way we think. God's Word is really powerful!

KEY TRUTH:

Meditate on the Word

Meditate on the Word
_____
_____
_____
_____
_____

Name: _____

Day: 1 ②3 4

<u>Copywork:</u> Copy Joshua 1:8 and think about how you can keep God's Word in your heart and mind. "Think about" is another way to say "meditate."

Meditate on it [the Word of God] day and night. (Joshua 1:8)

Read the poem.

Think About the Word

The Word of God is useful and good
The Bible says it's our heart's food.
It helps me focus on what's right
I'll think about it day and night.

When I'm feeling kind of mad
I know His Words can make me glad.
When I don't know what to do
The Word of God is alive and true.

I can trust the things I read.
I know that God will always lead
Me on the path that I should go,
And in His ways, to help me grow.

God's Word is my sword, to judge
   what is right.
His Word is a lamp, to shed new light.
His Word is a seed that produces
   fruit.
It is our foundation, to grow our
   roots.

Help me, Lord, to hear and obey,
To listen to the Words you say,
To everyday my mind renew
To think upon it through and through.

talk
about it!

What are some of the reasons the poem states that we should read God's Word?

WEEK 33: MEDITATE
ON THE WORD

CHARACTER STUDY

ATTENTIVE

Being attentive is what we are talking about this week. It means to listen or to be aware or observant. You can be attentive not just with your ears but with your heart, your eyes, and your mind. You are focused on what someone might be saying, doing, or feeling. You can be attentive to the Word of God, attentive when your pastor is speaking at church, and attentive to other people. James 1:19 tells us to be quick to hear and slow to speak. When we listen first, it helps us give not just any answer, but a wise answer! Have your parents ever told you to think before you speak?

Let's learn more about what it means to be attentive by looking at some synonyms and antonyms! From the list below, circle two of your favorite synonyms and antonyms for attentive.

Synonyms	Antonyms
alert	careless
listening	unaware
watchful	inconsiderate

Flash Card FUN
Make a flashcard with this week's character trait on it and decorate it however you want!

267

color it!

I AM ATTENTIVE

Name: _____

Day: 1 2 3 ④

draw it!

Different ways to meditate on the Word are to think about it, to sing about it, to write it out, or to talk about it. Can you show one of those ways by drawing a picture?

journal!

Name: _____

Day: 1 2 3 ④

Can you remember our key truth for the week?

_____
_____
_____
_____

Can you write or narrate to your parent or teacher what your picture is about?

_____
_____
_____
_____
_____
_____

 NOT ON MY OWN STRENGTH ...

Thank You, God, that You don't just hear me when I pray, You know me! You know how I am feeling and what I am thinking before I even tell You! Help me to learn to be more attentive to what You are saying!

 WEEK 33: MEDITATE ON THE WORD

Sometimes I get scared. I don't like the dark, and I don't like going into the basement by myself or when my brother shuts my door when I am in my room. Last night I had a bad dream and I woke up crying. Mom came into my room and we talked about what I had dreamed, and she said I needed to stop thinking about how scared I was. "Fear doesn't come from God," she told me. Sometimes when I am scared, I just keep thinking about what I am scared about over and over. Today, Mom read us a verse that told us to hold our thoughts like prisoners. I don't really do that all the time. I have lots of thoughts and I just think about whatever is in my mind, but the Bible tells us to control what we are thinking about. Last week, we learned how to think about God's Word, to think about things that are good and lovely. I want God to help me learn how to control my thoughts.

Malakai

Name: _____

Day: ① 2 3 4

talk about it!

Do you ever get scared?

What do you do when you are scared?

Check it with the Word!

We have learned to think about good things and meditate on the Word of God. We have also learned that the Bible is like a sword, and that it is powerful and good for discovering what is true and right. We have ALSO talked about how we need to test everything with the Word of God. Do you remember all that? All of those things are important to remember when we are thinking about our thoughts. Some of our thoughts are good, like when we are thinking about God or what we can do to help someone. But some of our thoughts are selfish or afraid or angry thoughts that we don't want to focus on. SO . . . when we are thinking about what we should do or what we want or how we are feeling, the Bible tells us to grab that thought and make it like a prisoner, trap it and test it with the Word of God.

Does it sound like something that is from God or something that we are supposed to be thinking about? If not, then we can start training our minds by choosing to think of something else instead! God can help us with this!

We destroy arguments and every lofty opinion raised against the knowledge of God, and take every thought captive to obey Christ. (2 Corinthians 10:5)

KEY TRUTH:

Take every thought captive

Take every thought captive
_____
_____
_____
_____

Copywork: Copy this verse and think about how you can you can take your thoughts captive today.

Take every thought captive to obey
Christ. (2 Corinthians 10:5)

Paul in Prison by Rembrandt van Rijn (1627)

Art study

This is a painting of Paul, the man who wrote some of the New Testament of the Bible from a prison cell. Paul spent lots of time in prison, and he is the one who wrote 2 Corinthians, the letter to the church in Corinth where we read to "take every thought captive." He knew what it meant to be captive, to be a prisoner. He probably had lots of time to think, to be worried or feel sorry for himself, but he was learning to test his thoughts. Notice the sword by his bed? Sometimes artists use symbols or objects to represent meaning. Maybe the sword is there to remind us of the sword of the Spirit, the Word of God.

LET'S LOOK CLOSER

Where do you think the light is coming from? Can you see the little corner of the window at the top?

What do you think Paul is writing?

Does he look scared or angry? Thoughtful or happy?

What are some of the colors you see in the painting?

How does this painting make you feel?

RESPONSIBLE

Name: _____

Day: 1 2 ③ 4

Being responsible means that you do the things you say you will or that you know you should, and that you accept the consequences of your actions. Can you think of an example of how you can be responsible? Some ideas are doing your chores, or if you make a mistake, telling your parents and being willing to take the punishment. Being responsible might be taking care of your bike and putting it away or not losing something that was entrusted to you. There are lots of ways that we can be responsible.

Let's look at some synonyms and antonyms of **responsible** to help us learn what it means.

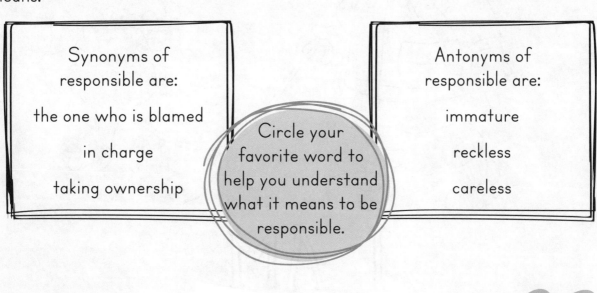

Synonyms of responsible are:

the one who is blamed

in charge

taking ownership

Circle your favorite word to help you understand what it means to be responsible.

Antonyms of responsible are:

immature

reckless

careless

Flash Card FUN

Make a flashcard with this week's character trait on it and decorate it however you want!

WEEK 34: TAKE EVERY THOUGHT CAPTIVE

Name: _____

Day: 1 2 ③ 4

color it!

I AM RESPONSIBLE

Name: _____

Day: 1 2 3 ④

draw it!

Draw a picture of you doing something that is responsible.

journal!

Name: _____

Day: 1 2 3 ④

Can you remember our key truth for the week?

_____
_____
_____
_____

Can you write or narrate to your parent/teacher a thought that you should take captive?

_____
_____
_____
_____
_____
_____

NOT ON MY OWN STRENGTH . . .

Father, thank You that you showed us the very best example of someone who was responsible. Thank You, Jesus, for dying on the Cross, for taking all my punishment, even when it wasn't Yours to take! Help me to grow to be more responsible, more trustworthy, and more mature in You!

We went to the playground today and I made some new friends! One of the girls said some bad words and was not being very nice to her mom and brother. But she was really nice to me and she shared her snack and we were talking and hiding from the other kids under the slide. Every time someone tried to come and play with us, my new friend would tell them they weren't allowed in. Even my little sister tried, and she said no, and Janiah started crying and went to my mom.

In the car afterward, my mom and I were talking about making good choices — that the people we are friends with and want to be like should be people that make us better, not people that make us act in ways we know are wrong. I said sorry to Janiah for leaving her out and am going to try really hard to not change who I am just to be liked by someone else.

Aliyah

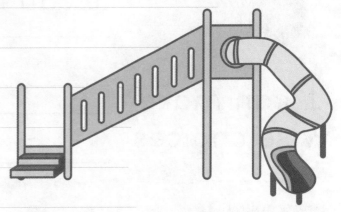

Name: _____

Day: ① 2 3 4

talk about it!

Why do you think Aliyah was being like her friend and not letting people play with them?

Do you ever try to act like your friends so they will like you?

What makes a good friend?

Check it with the Word!

BIBLE

Do not be deceived: "Bad company ruins good morals." (1 Corinthians 15:33)

Do you know what morals are? Morals are the things that you believe are right — your standards, the way that you live your life. If you believe that you should be truthful and not lie, that is a moral. The way that you choose to spend your time, the songs that you listen to, the movies that you watch, the friends that you spend time with . . . all of those things help feed who you are and what you believe and how you act. If you are trying to be like a friend more than doing what is right, then you let go of your morals. One of the ways that we can worship God and include Him every day is by honoring Him with the way we live our lives and the choices we make. Asking His advice, living with integrity, and making good choices that we know He tells us in the Bible are all ways we worship God and have a relationship with Him.

KEY TRUTH:

I can make wise choices

I can make wise choices
_____
_____
_____
_____
_____

Copywork: Write out the following verse and let God write it on your heart.

Bad company ruins good morals.

(1 Corinthians 15:33)

Name: _____

Day: 1 ② 3 4

Read this song out loud slowly and think about the words.

BE THOU MY VISION

Hymn: verse two	➡	Interpretation:
Be Thou my Wisdom, and Thou my true Word;	～	Help me be wise and to come to you for truth
I ever with Thee and Thou with me, Lord;	～	I want you to be with me always
Thou my great Father, I Thy true son;	～	You are my great Father and I am your child
Thou in me dwelling, and I with Thee one.	～	Your Spirit is in me we are one

talk about it!

This hymn is about God being everything — what we think about, our wisdom, with us, our protector, our treasure, our Father, etc. What do you think it means for God to be our wisdom?

Listen through the song with your parent or teacher and circle or highlight the rhyming words.

You can explore this entire hymn with a line-by-line modern interpretation pages 317-318.

WEEK 35: MAKING WISE CHOICES

CHARACTER STUDY

SINCERE

To be sincere is kind of like being honest all the way in your heart: to act from something you feel with your whole heart. An example would be if you said sorry to your friend and you didn't really mean it, you aren't being sincere. If you say sorry and you really mean it, then you are being sincere . . . you actually feel and believe what you are saying. Joshua 24:14 tells us to fear the Lord and serve Him in sincerity and in faithfulness. We want our faith to be sincere, something we really believe and feel and know, all the way in our hearts!

Let's learn more about what it means to be **sincere** by looking at some similar words (synonyms) and opposite words (antonyms). Copy two of your favorite in the correct column.

Synonym		Antonym	
heartfelt)		false)	
real)		not true)	
true)		dishonest)	

Flash Card FUN
Make a flashcard with this week's character trait on it and decorate it however you want!

283

I am sincere

Name: _____

Day: 1 2 3 ④

draw it!

Do you have a really good friend? Someone you admire or is a good example? Draw a picture of you together.

WEEK 35: MAKING
WISE CHOICES

journal!

Name: _____

Day: 1 2 3 ④

Can you remember our key truth for the week?

_____
- -
_____
_____
- -
_____

Write or narrate to your teacher what your drawing is about and how it can help you remember to make wise choices.

_____
- -
_____
_____
- -
_____
_____
- -
_____

NOT ON MY OWN STRENGTH...

Jesus, help me to be more sincere in my faith in You, in how I serve You, in the way I love others. Thank You that You are helping me grow my character just by being with You. Thank You for helping me be who You want me to become.

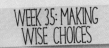

We have learned SO much about our great relationship with God, but we don't want to forget it! Each week, you have learned a key truth! Today, we are going to play a game to help us remember what they are.

Pull out pages 331-333 for Quarter 4 and cut out your Key Truth cards. There are lots of ways to help you remember your key truths. You can hop on each card and try to remember what it is or say what it means to you. You can ask a parent to read the first part and see if you can remember the end. You can copy them out and you can decorate them! Think of a fun way you can review your key truths!

If you have been working on your character trait flashcards, this is the week you get to practice them all together! There are so many fun ways to do this! You can practice them on your own by just reading them through or you can play a game to make it more fun! You can even play a game with a family member or friend. You can take turns reading the character trait and have the other person say an example, act it out, or explain what it means. Then trade places! You can make another copy of your cards (or have a parent help) and play memory by turning them all over and trying to find matching pairs. You can even put them on the floor in a pattern or build an obstacle course and as you find the cards or land on the cards, say what it is or what it means OR an example of that character trait.

SO many fun ways to review your cards! Choose one or make up your own and see how well you can remember what these character traits look like in action!

Name: _____

Day: 1 (2) 3 4

Highlight, circle, or color the words in the puzzle below.

F	A	I	R	R	S	H	G	T	O	R	N
S	K	N	E	A	P	P	B	L	E	L	V
I	L	M	S	T	I	F	S	A	V	D	J
N	M	O	P	T	C	H	I	C	C	B	J
C	S	R	O	E	O	E	N	G	G	O	P
E	Y	U	N	N	N	L	T	I	Y	T	P
R	W	F	S	T	F	P	E	V	Q	W	P
E	C	L	I	I	I	F	G	I	W	Z	Q
N	T	P	B	V	D	U	R	N	K	H	V
Y	R	V	L	E	E	L	I	G	N	N	A
T	G	Z	E	V	N	Z	T	U	L	F	Y
I	C	S	E	P	T	U	Y	S	M	H	W

ATTENTIVE   GIVING   RESPONSIBLE

CONFIDENT   HELPFUL   SINCERE

FAIR   INTEGRITY

WEEK 36: REVIEW

288

To help us reflect on what we have learned about this quarter, we are going to do a creative connection, or artistic, hands-on project! This is optional. If you prefer, you can draw a picture or use playdough or something to show what you learned.

LET'S CONNECT creatively

WHOLE FAMILY ACTIVITY

Living Close to God

Supplies needed:

- a Bible journal or poster board (you decide how big you want it)

- pencil/pencil crayons/markers

Instructions: Today we are going to do a project to help us remember that God is with us ALWAYS, and that He wants us to pray without ceasing. That means He wants us to talk to Him all the time, about everything! On the poster board, write at the very top: God is with me and wants to talk to me when . . .

Underneath, draw some pictures of things you do throughout your day:

I brush my teeth

I make my bed

I do my chores

I do my school work

I eat my food

I play with my friends

I watch a show

I read a book

God is with you all the time, every day, and He wants to be your friend! Every time you spend time with Him, pray, think about Him, think about His Words, or do what the Bible says, you are worshiping Him and growing stronger in your faith!

WEEK 36: REVIEW

journal!

What is your strongest character trait?

Which one do you need to work on the most?

What is your favorite thing you learned about being a Christian?

Congratulations!

You finished your journey for Volume I with Malakai and Aliyah. On the following page is a special completion form you can fill out and hang up, if you like. It is my hope and prayer that you have a better understanding of who God is, who He made you to be, and what it means to have a relationship with Him. As you continue your adventure with Jesus, ask a parent or teacher to read this prayer over you:

May God
complete the good work
He has started in you. May He
reveal Himself to you in new ways and
draw you close to Him. May you follow
Him all the days of your life. May you grow
in His ways and be marked as His child and
know your true identity in Him, not in the world
or the people around you. May your faith run deep
and you build your house upon the rock and have a
firm foundation in this culture of shifting sands.
And may you be a warrior in the Lord's army,
prepared for battle, with the full armor
of God to protect you, a generation of
children who see truth.

Amen

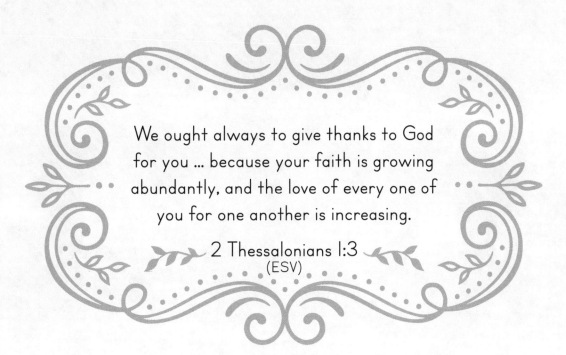

We ought always to give thanks to God for you ... because your faith is growing abundantly, and the love of every one of you for one another is increasing.

2 Thessalonians 1:3
(ESV)

This acknowledges that

_____

has completed *More Than Words Level 1*

on

_____

We give thanks for your growth!

Master Books®

Appendices

FULL HYMNS
REVIEW CARDS

THE LOVE OF GOD
Frederick Lehman

Hymn: verse one	Interpretation:
The love of God is greater far	The love of God is better
Than tongue or pen can ever tell	Than anyone can say or write
It goes beyond the highest star	It is higher than the stars
And reaches to the lowest hell	always there no matter how far away from God you are.
The guilty pair, bowed down with care	For everyone that is guilty
God gave His Son to win	God gave His Son, Jesus, to defeat sin
His erring child He reconciled	God's sinful child (us), He made right again
And pardoned from his sin	And forgave his sin

verse two

When hoary time shall pass away,	When ancient time passes by
And earthly thrones and kingdoms fall;	And kings and kingdoms fall
When men who here refuse to pray,	When men who will not pray
On rocks and hills and mountains call;	Call on the hills and mountains
God's love, so sure shall still endure,	God's love will still be there
All measureless and strong;	Strong and without limits
Redeeming grace to Adam's race—	Saving grace to man
The saint's and angel's song.	The saint's and angels song

verse three

Could we with ink the ocean fill,	If we could fill the oceans with ink
And were the skies of parchment made,	And if the skies were paper
Were every stalk on earth a quill	If every plant on earth was a pen
And every man a scribe by trade;	And every single man on earth a writer
To write the love of God above	To write the love of God on the paper of the sky
Would drain the ocean dry;	Would drain the entire ocean of ink
Nor could the scroll contain the whole,	The paper couldn't hold his love
Tho' stretched from sky to sky.	Even though it was the whole sky

chorus

Oh love of God, how rich and pure!	God's love is so rich and perfect
How measureless and strong!	Strong, with no end
It shall forevermore endure,	It will be there forever
The saint's and angels song.	It is the song of the saint's and the angels

23RD PSALM
King David

Hymn: verse one		Interpretation:
The Lord's my shepherd, I'll not want;		The Lord is my shepherd, I will not want anything else
He makes me down to lie		He makes me lay down
In pastures green; he leadeth me		In green fields, he leads me
The quiet waters by.		To quiet waters (this is a peaceful place)

verse two

My soul he doth restore again,		He fixes my soul
And me to walk doth make		And makes me walk
Within the paths of righteousness,		The way I should
E'en for his own name's sake.		For His name's sake

verse three

Yea, though I walk in death's dark vale,		Even when I am touched by death's shadow (maybe someone in your life dies)
Yet will I fear no ill:		I will fear nothing bad
For thou art with me, and thy rod		Because you are with me, and your rod
And staff me comfort still.		And your staff (the tools of a shepherd), comfort me

verse four

My table thou hast furnished		You set a table
In presence of my foes;		In front of my enemies
My head thou dost with oil anoint		You put oil on my head
And my cup overflows.		And I am filled until I spill

Goodness and mercy all my life	∼	Goodness and mercy will follow me
Shall surely follow me;	∼	All of my life
And in God's house for evermore	∼	And I will forever be
My dwelling-place shall be.	∼	In God's house

JUST A CLOSER WALK WITH THEE

author unknown

Hymn: verse one		Interpretation:
I am weak but Thou art strong;		I am weak but you are strong
Jesus, keep me from all wrong;		Jesus help me not to sin
I'll be satisfied as long		I'll be happy as long
As I walk, let me walk close to Thee.		As I walk close to you

refrain

Just a closer walk with Thee,		I want to walk closer to you
Grant it, Jesus, is my plea,		This is my prayer
Daily walking close to Thee,		Walking close with you every day
Let it be, dear Lord, let it be.		Let it happen

verse two

Thro' this world of toil and snares,		Life is difficult and dangerous
If I falter, Lord, who cares?		But if I fall down or make a mistake, who cares?
Who with me my burden shares?		Who helps me when I am struggling?
None but Thee, dear Lord, none but Thee.		No one but you Jesus.

verse three

When my feeble life is o'er,		When my life is over
Time for me will be no more;		And my time is up
Guide me gently, safely o'er		Guide me safely and gently
To Thy kingdom shore, to Thy shore.		To heaven

DO YOU KNOW THAT YOU WERE CHOSEN
Charles Crozat Converse

Hymn: verse one	Interpretation:
Do you know that you were chosen	Do you know that you were chosen
Long before the world began	Before the world was made
That by God you were selected	That God chose you
And appointed for His plan?	And gave you a job
Something in your inmost being	Something inside you
Tells you this is surely true;	Tells you this must be true
That's why you are in this meeting,	That is why you are here (church)
And you feel the way you do.	And why you feel the way you do

verse two

All the sins you've e'er committed,	All the sins you have done
Everything you've ever done,	Everything bad, every mistake
All by God has been forgiven	Has been forgiven by God
Taken care of by God's Son.	Taken care of by Jesus
Struggle not, no; just believe this,	Don't worry, just believe it
For His word assures it's true;	Because the Bible tells us it is true
All you need to do is thank Him	All you need to do is thank Him
For all that He's done for you.	For everything He's done for you

verse three

Did you know that all the Bible	Do you know that the Bible
Is a will, a testament?	Is proof, the true story
Everything that Christ accomplished	Of everything Jesus did
Is for all God's children meant.	For all His children

303

As His child you are included,	You are one of His children
For His word stands fast and true;	For His word (the Bible) is true
So by faith you now inherit	So by faith you now have
All that He has done for you.	The same gift of salvation

verse four

Did you know God has a family?	Do you know God has a family?
Yes, He does, in fact, it's us.	Yes, we are His family
That's why we are here enjoying	That is why we are here
All He is, so marvelous.	Enjoying who He is
He's our God and we're His people,	He is our God, we are His people
Day by day we love Him more;	We love Him more everyday
We're so happy and so thankful,	We're so happy and thankful
We just praise Him o'er and o'er.	We praise Him again and again

verse five

All we know is that we love Him,	All we know is that we love Him
We're so glad for what He's done;	And are so glad for what He's done
We are brought to Him, and we all	We are brought to Him
Know the joy of being one.	And know what it means to be part of His family
We're so glad that we're included,	We're so glad that we're a part
What a fellowship have we!	What a special connection we have
So we'd like to welcome you, friend,	So we'd like to welcome you
Into God's own family.	Into God's own family

TAKE MY LIFE AND LET IT BE
Frances Ridley Havergal

Hymn: verse one	⟹	Interpretation:
Take my life, and let it be		Take my life and let it be
Consecrated, Lord, to Thee;		Declared "I am God's"
Take my moments and my days,		Take every moment, every day
Let them flow in ceaseless praise,		Let them be filled with praise
Let them flow in ceaseless praise.		Let them be filled with praise

verse two

Take my hands, and let them move		Take my hands and let them be
At the impulse of Thy love;		Used by Your love
Take my feet, and let them be		Take my feet and let them be
Swift and beautiful for Thee,		Fast and walking where You tell me
Swift and beautiful for Thee.		Fast and walking where You tell me

verse three

Take my voice and let me sing		I give You my voice, let me sing
Always only for my King;		For You, my King (God)
Take my lips, and let them be		I give You my lips, let my mouth be
Filled with messages from Thee,		Filled with Your words
Filled with messages from Thee.		Filled with Your words

verse four

Take my silver and my gold,	∼	Take my money
Not a mite would I withhold:	∼	I won't hold any of it back from you
Take my intellect, and use	∼	Take my mind, my thoughts, my smarts
Ev'ry pow'r as Thou shalt choose,	∼	And use it as You want
Ev'ry pow'r as Thou shalt choose.	∼	And use it as You want

verse five

Take my will, and make it Thine;	∼	Take what I want and make it what You want
It shall be no longer mine:	∼	I give it to You
Take my heart, it is Thine own;	∼	Take my heart, it is Yours
It shall be Thy royal throne,	∼	You are the King of my heart
It shall be Thy royal throne.	∼	Be the King of my heart

verse six

Take my love, my Lord, I pour	∼	Take my love, my Lord, I pour
At Thy feet its treasure store:	∼	I pour my love and desires at Your feet
Take myself, and I will be	∼	Take all that I am and I will be
Ever, only, all for Thee,	∼	Only ever Yours
Ever, only, all for Thee.	∼	Only ever Yours

MY FAITH LOOKS UP TO THEE

Ray Palmer

Hymn: verse one	Interpretation:
My faith looks up to Thee,	My faith trusts in You
Thou Lamb of Calvary,	The Lamb who died on the cross
Saviour Divine;	Perfect Savior
Now hear me while I pray;	Hear me while I pray
Take all my guilt away;	Take away my sin
Oh, let me from this day	Let me, from today
Be wholly Thine.	Be all Yours

verse two

May Thy rich grace impart	Give me Your grace
Strength to my fainting heart	Give my heart strength
My zeal inspire;	Inspire my will
As Thou hast died for me,	As You have died for me
Oh, may my love to Thee	May my love for You
Pure, warm, and changeless be,	Be pure, warm and unchanging
A living fire	A living fire

While life's dark maze I tread,	~	When life is confusing
And griefs around me spread,	~	And hard and sad
Be Thou my Guide;	~	Be my guide
Bid darkness turn to day,	~	Make the dark times be light
Wipe sorrow's tears away,	~	Wipe away my sadness
Nor let me ever stray	~	Don't let me ever go the wrong way
From Thee aside.	~	Never away from You

verse four

All thru life's transient dream,	~	All through my life
Until death's sullen stream	~	Until I the day
Shall o'er me roll,	~	That I die
Blest Saviour, with Thy love,	~	God, with Your love
Fear and distrust remove;	~	Take away all my fear and distrust
Make me Thy grace to prove	~	Make me proof of Your grace
Transform my soul.	~	Change me

SWEET HOUR OF PRAYER
Donna K. Maltese

Hymn: verse one		Interpretation:
Sweet hour of prayer! Sweet hour of prayer!		Sweet hour of prayer Sweet hour of prayer
That calls me from a world of care,		That calls me from my worries
And bids me at my Father's throne		And says "Come to God's throne"
Make all my wants and wishes known.		And tell Him what you want
In seasons of distress and grief,		In hard times, in sad times
My soul has often found relief,		My soul finds rest
And oft escaped the tempter's snare,		I have often escaped temptation
By thy return, sweet hour of prayer!		Through prayer

verse two

Sweet hour of prayer! Sweet hour of prayer!		Sweet hour of prayer Sweet hour of prayer
The joys I feel, the bliss I share,		I feel joy and happiness
Of those whose anxious spirits burn		With those whose hearts burn
With strong desires for thy return!		With a longing to see God
With such I hasten to the place		With those people I go quickly to the place
Where God my Savior shows His face,		Where God shows his face
And gladly take my station there,		I stay in that place
And wait for thee, sweet hour of prayer!		And wait for you in prayer

verse three

Sweet hour of prayer! Sweet hour of prayer!	Sweet hour of prayer Sweet hour of prayer
Thy wings shall my petition bear	That calls me from my worries
To Him whose truth and faithfulness	And says "Come to God's throne"
Engage the waiting soul to bless.	And tell Him what you want
And since He bids me seek His face,	In hard times, in sad times
Believe His Word and trust His grace	My soul finds rest
I'll cast on Him my every care,	I have often escaped temptation
And wait for thee, sweet hour of prayer!	Through prayer

verse four

Sweet hour of prayer! Sweet hour of prayer!	Sweet hour of prayer Sweet hour of prayer
May I thy consolation share,	May I find comfort there
Till, from Mount Pisgah's lofty height,	Until from the top of Mount Pisgah (the mountain Moses first saw the Promised Land)
I view my home and take my flight.	I view heaven and leave this earth
This robe of flesh I'll drop, and rise	I leave my body and rise to heaven
To seize the everlasting prize,	To receive my prize (eternal life)
And shout, while passing through the air, "Farewell, farewell, sweet hour of prayer!"	And shout while I fly through the air Goodbye, goodbye, sweet hour of prayer

VICTORY IN JESUS
Eugene Monroe Bartlett, Sr.

Hymn: verse one	Interpretation:
I heard an old, old story,	I heard an old story
How a Savior came from glory,	How Someone came to save us
How He gave His life on Calvary	How He died on the Cross
To save a wretch like me;	To save a sinner like me
I heard about His groaning,	I heard about His sadness
Of His precious blood's atoning	And how His blood saved us
Then I repented of my sins;	Then I said, "I am sorry for my sins"
And won the victory.	And I won eternal life!

refrain

O victory in Jesus,	Victory in Jesus
My Savior, forever.	My Savior forever
He sought me and bought me	He looked for me and bought me
With His redeeming blood;	With His saving blood
He loved me ere I knew Him,	He loved be before I even knew Him
And all my love is due Him,	And I owe Him all my love
He plunged me to victory,	He dunked me into victory
Beneath the cleansing flood	With His cleaning flood

verse two

I heard about His healing,	～	I heard about His healing
Of His cleansing power revealing.	～	Of His power to take my sin away
How He made the lame to walk again	～	How He made people who could not walk walk again
And caused the blind to see;	～	And gave the blind their sight
And then I cried, "Dear Jesus,	～	And then I cried, "Dear Jesus"
Come and heal my broken spirit,"	～	"Come and heal my broken spirit,"
And somehow Jesus came and brought	～	And somehow Jesus came and brought
To me the victory.	～	Me victory

verse three

I heard about a mansion	～	I heard about a huge house
He has built for me in glory.	～	That He built for me in heaven
And I heard about the streets of gold	～	I heard about the streets of gold
Beyond the crystal sea;	～	Beyond the crystal sea
About the angels singing,	～	About the angels singing
And the old redemption story,	～	And the story of the cross
And some sweet day I'll sing up there	～	And some sweet day I'll sing in heaven
The song of victory.	～	The song of victory

SEEK YE FIRST
Karen Lafferty

Hymn: verse one		Interpretation:
Seek ye first the Kingdom of God		Chase after God's kingdom first, before anything else
And His righteousness		And His righteousness
And all these things shall be added unto you		And all these things will be given to you
Allelu Alleluia		Praise God

verse two

Man shall not live by bread alone		Man does not live by just bread
But by every word		But by every word
That proceeds from the mouth of God		From God's mouth
Allelu Alleluia		Praise God

verse three

Ask and it shall be given unto you		Ask and you will get it
Seek and ye shall find		Look and you will find it
Knock and the door shall be opened unto you		Knock and the door will open
Allelu Alleluia		Praise God

chorus

Al - le - lu - ia		Praise God
Al - le - lu - ia		Praise God
Al - le - lu - ia		Praise God
Al - le - lu Al - le - lu - ia		Praise God

THOU TRUE VINE, THAT HEALS THE NATIONS

Percy Dearmer

Hymn: verse one	Interpretation:
Thou true Vine, that heals the nations,	You are the Vine that heals us
Tree of life, thy branches we.	You are the Tree of the Life, we are the branches
They who leave thee fade and wither,	Those who leave You, are like leaves that change and dry in the fall
none bear fruit except in thee.	We only produce fruit with You
Cleanse us, make us sane and simple,	Clean us, renew our minds
till we merge our lives in thine,	Until we live like You, with You
gain ourselves in thee, the Vintage,	We find ourselves in You, the Source
give ourselves through thee, the Vine.	Use us, through You—the Vine

verse two

Nothing can we do without thee;	We can't do anything without You
on thy life depends each one.	We depend on You
If we keep thy words and love thee,	If we obey and love You
all we ask for shall be done.	We will get everything we ask for
May we, loving one another,	May we love each other
radiant in thy light abide;	And stay in Your light
so through us, made fruitful by thee,	Help us to produce fruit in our lives
shall our God be glorified.	To glorify God

BE THOU MY VISION
Dallán Forgaill

Hymn: verse one Interpretation:

Hymn: verse one	Interpretation:
Be Thou my Vision, O Lord of my heart;	Be what I look to, Lord of my heart
Naught be all else to me, save that Thou art;	Let there be nothing but You
Thou my best Thought, by day or by night,	Be what I think about day and night
Waking or sleeping, Thy presence my light.	Whether I am sleeping or awake, Your presence be with me.

verse two

Be Thou my Wisdom, and Thou my true Word;	Help me be wise and to come to You for truth
I ever with Thee and Thou with me, Lord;	I want You to be with me always
Thou my great Father, I Thy true son;	You are my great Father and I am Your child
Thou in me dwelling, and I with Thee one.	Your Spirit is in me, we are one

verse three

Be Thou my battle Shield, Sword for the fight;	Be my shield, my sword
Be Thou my Dignity, Thou my Delight;	Be my dignity and what I find joy in
Thou my soul's Shelter, Thou my high Tow'r:	You are my soul's safe place, my safe tower
Raise Thou me heav'nward, O Pow'r of my pow'r.	Raise me to heaven, powerful God

Riches I heed not,
nor man's empty praise,

I don't care about being rich or
what people say about me

Thou mine Inheritance,
now and always:

Be mine forever

Thou and Thou only,
first in my heart,

You only, the most important
thing in my heart

High King of Heaven,
my Treasure Thou art.

High King of Heaven,
You are my treasure

verse five

High King of Heaven,
my victory won,

High King of Heaven, You won

May I reach Heaven's joys,
O bright Heav'n's Sun!

May I reach Heaven

Heart of my own heart,
whatever befall,

Whatever may happen

Still be my Vision, O Ruler of all.

Be what I look to, O Ruler of all.

KEY TRUTH:

God is 3 in 1

KEY TRUTH:

God is love

KEY TRUTH:

God is good

KEY TRUTH:

God is eternal

Quarter 1 Key Truth Cards

KEY TRUTH:

God is always with me

KEY TRUTH:

God is beyond understanding

KEY TRUTH:

God knows everything

KEY TRUTH:

God is the great I Am

KEY TRUTH:

I am created
and loved

KEY TRUTH:

No one is
perfect

KEY TRUTH:

God
chose me

KEY TRUTH:

I am saved
by Jesus

323

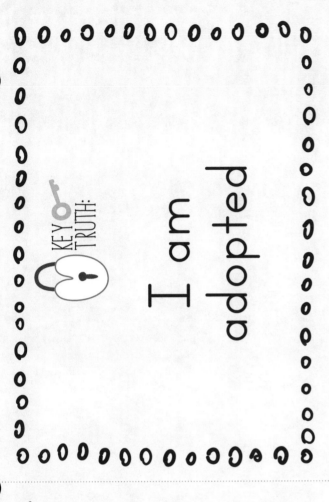

KEY TRUTH:

I am
adopted

KEY TRUTH:

I am an
imitator of God

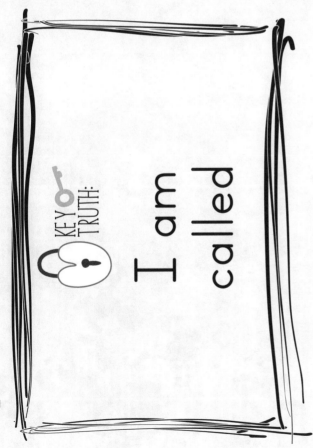

KEY TRUTH:

I am
called

KEY TRUTH:

I am who God
says I am

KEY TRUTH:

I can talk to God

KEY TRUTH:

God's Word is powerful

KEY TRUTH:

I can worship God

KEY TRUTH:

Faith without works is dead

Quarter 3 Key Truth Cards

KEY TRUTH:
God gives gifts

KEY TRUTH:
The Holy Spirit helps me

KEY TRUTH:
I follow God's commands

KEY TRUTH:
Put on the armor of God

329

Quarter 3 Key Truth Cards

KEY TRUTH:

God speaks to me

KEY TRUTH:

Seek and you will find

KEY TRUTH:

God wants me close

KEY TRUTH:

Pray all the time

Quarter 4 Key Truth Cards

KEY TRUTH:

My roots are in Jesus

KEY TRUTH:

Meditate on the Word

KEY TRUTH:

Take every thought captive

KEY TRUTH:

I can make wise choices

> "**THANKS TO MASTER BOOKS, OUR YEAR IS GOING SO SMOOTHLY!**"
> — SHAINA

Made for "Real World" Homeschooling

FAITH-BUILDING

We ensure that a biblical worldview is integral to all of our curriculum. We start with the Bible as our standard and build our courses from there. We strive to demonstrate biblical teachings and truth in all subjects.

TRUSTED

We've been publishing quality Christian books for over 40 years. We publish best-selling Christian authors like Henry Morris, Ken Ham, and Ray Comfort.

EFFECTIVE

We use experienced educators to create our curriculum for real-world use. We don't just teach knowledge by itself. We also teach how to apply and use that knowledge.

ENGAGING

We make our curriculum fun and inspire a joy for learning. We go beyond rote memorization by emphasizing hands-on activities and real-world application.

PRACTICAL

We design our curriculum to be so easy that you can open the box and start homeschooling. We provide easy-to-use schedules and pre-planned lessons that make education easy for busy homeschooling families.

FLEXIBLE

We create our material to be readily adaptable to any homeschool program. We know that one size does not fit all and that homeschooling requires materials that can be customized for your family's wants and needs.

VISIT **MASTERBOOKS.COM** — *Where Faith Grows!* — TO SEE OUR FULL LINE OF FAITH-BUILDING CURRICULUM OR CALL 800-999-3777.

LET'S *GET* SOCIAL

@ nah_yu

@welcometoourcabin

@ dawn.santoro